Chronology of the Stock Market

Chronology
of the
Stock Market

RUSSELL O. WRIGHT

McFarland & Company, Inc., Publishers
Jefferson, North Carolina, and London

Library of Congress cataloguing data are available;

ISBN 0-7864-1328-X (softcover : 60# alkaline paper) ∞

British Library cataloguing data are available

Cover photograph © 2001 www.comstock.com

Manufactured in the United States of America

*McFarland & Company, Inc., Publishers
Box 611, Jefferson, North Carolina 28640
www.mcfarlandpub.com*

To Terry Ann Wright

CONTENTS

ACKNOWLEDGMENTS

Writing a book of this type requires many references. I have listed the most important of those references in my bibliography in the end pages of the book. But I want to especially acknowledge the resources of the New York Stock Exchange. Not only is their website filled with useful reference information, the book they authorized as part of the celebration of their 200th Anniversary, *The New York Stock Exchange, The First 200 Years*, was of enormous help in assembling a chronology such as this. Their book is included in my bibliography, and I have also added an author's note in my book recommending that readers consult the NYSE book for more detail about the construction of their present building that was completed in 1903 (and its addition that was completed in 1922). I did not have enough space to do this subject justice.

I want especially to thank my daughter, Terry Ann Wright, who did most of the work at the computer keyboard now that a stroke has forced my return to the "hunt-and-peck" method of typing. But beyond her word processing skills and her ability to type a bazillion words per minute, I want to acknowledge her help in choosing just the right word, as well as her suggestions that helped to eliminate those "what in the world is this supposed to mean" phrases. Beyond doing the basic research for the book, it's hard to imagine that any co-author could have done more than she did in making the book ready for publication.

INTRODUCTION

This Chronology deals with stock markets in the United States only. As a practical matter, a good part of the book is devoted to the New York Stock Exchange (NYSE). The NYSE, for most of its existence, has been much bigger than all the other stock exchanges in the United States combined. Thus the history of the stock market in the United States is largely the history of the NYSE. The terms "stock market" and "stock exchange" usually are used interchangeably, but a stock exchange has a trading floor (or several) where stocks listed on that exchange are traded. Only certain stocks with substantial size and some history can meet the stringent requirements to be listed on a major exchange such as the NYSE. Thus, a history of even an exchange as large as the NYSE is a history of only a limited number (a little over 3,000 today) of stocks. The term stock market actually refers to all of the exchanges and the rest of the marketplace where stocks that cannot meet the exchange listing requirements are bought and sold. In the United States, the stocks that are not traded on an exchange have been, and are, traded on what is called the over-the-counter (OTC) market.

The OTC stock market means almost precisely what it says. If a stock was not listed on an exchange, one had to go to the company that issues the stock and buy it directly "over the counter," or one had to go to a dealer who keeps an inventory of various stocks and sells them "over the counter" in the same way one would sell a slice of ham. The OTC market is extremely large in terms of the numbers of companies that are sold there, but historically these companies have not been able to meet the listing requirements to be sold on an exchange, which means they are generally smaller and are riskier investments.

In the United States, this all changed in 1971 when the Nasdaq stock market began operation. As is pointed out in detail in the book, the National Association of Securities Dealers (NASD) was an organization of OTC brokers. When the NASD, with government encouragement and support, created the NASDAQ stock market in 1971 (the acronym initially just added "AQ" for Automated Quotation to the NASD acronym, but now the Nasdaq is no longer considered an acronym and just simply stands for itself), it created a stock market that would not only become competitive with, but in some ways surpass, the NYSE. The Nasdaq did not, however, have any trading floors, as all stock exchanges all over the world did at the time. The "trading floor" of the Nasdaq were the thousands of computer terminals located in the brokerage offices that either belonged to the NASD or subscribed to the Nasdaq stock market. This means that although the Nasdaq is now a huge stock market, it is not, in the traditional sense, a stock exchange.

One advantage of a stock exchange in the sense of trading stocks is that the stocks need to meet some minimum economic requirements to be listed in the first place, as noted above. Another advantage is that, with thousands of members belonging to an exchange like the NYSE, you get a marketplace that really represents a true auction and you can be sure of getting the best price when you are buying or selling a stock on an exchange.

However, in a system such as the Nasdaq, which started out with only a limited number of market makers, the "auction" price for buying or selling was the price made up by perhaps as few as one trader on a single stock. More popular stocks may have had several traders making the Nasdaq market, but it was not nearly as effective as the process that took place on the floor of the NYSE. The limited number of dealers in the Nasdaq marketplace made it easier to manipulate the market. And for many years, the OTC market had a poor reputation. It has overcome that reputation to some extent now that the number of companies belonging to the Nasdaq outnumber those belonging to the NYSE (the book shows that this is an inevitable result of a government law), and the volume of trading now regularly exceeds that of the NYSE. But the number of market makers is not guaranteed, and there still is the small odor of a pool hall hanging over the Nasdaq market. We examine some of the reasons for this in the book.

However, this book will show that the Nasdaq market has deservedly taken its place among the top few markets in the world, and negative feelings about it have diminished. Unfortunately, the aftermaths of the overall stock market crash of 1987, and the Nasdaq market crash in the year 2000, have shown that the odor has not completely disappeared.

This means that, after 1971, when we talk about the stock market in the United States in this book, we are talking about two different markets: the NYSE and the Nasdaq. These markets completely overshadow all other markets in the United States by sizable margins. In fact, by picking these two markets as those representing the United States, we are actually picking the two top markets in the entire world at present. The NYSE has been the number one market in the world since World War I ended and the NYSE took over for the London market as the top place in the world to raise capital. In the late 1980s, the Tokyo stock market for a short time exceeded the total capitalization of the NYSE or the Nasdaq. But after the Tokyo stock market bubble burst in 1989, the NYSE and the Nasdaq moved back on top. So in focusing on "just" the NYSE and the Nasdaq, we actually are focusing on the top international markets as well (some of which have started "electronic" exchanges copying the Nasdaq example).

To summarize, this book will track the chronology of the NYSE from its beginnings in 1792, and will track the chronology of both the NYSE and the Nasdaq from 1971, although it will also include earlier milestones for the OTC market, which has been in existence as long as people have traded stocks (or anything else, for that matter). These two markets are justifiably the focus of the book because they represent together by far the biggest "stock market" in the universe. Once we reach the 1990s, we will concentrate on the milestones of the values of the Dow Jones averages (which in a way primarily represent the NYSE), and the values of the Nasdaq index, as these two indexes climbed toward their peaks, with both markets now on reasonably equal footing.

By the year 2000, the differences between the two markets had begun to blur. The Nasdaq had become successful enough to acquire the old American Stock Exchange (AMEX), and much of the trading in the nation and the world was beginning to focus on such financial products as futures rather than stocks. This was important because stock markets were becoming increasingly interconnected. Thus, there are fewer developmental milestones to report for both markets. However, there was much discussion about why the Nasdaq crashed, and what the various brokers and brokerages should do about it.

I have mentioned the crash of the Nasdaq in 2001, and the bursting of the Tokyo stock market bubble in 1989. Actually, the Nasdaq crash might better be called the bursting of a bubble as well. In essence, the difference between a "crash" and the bursting of a "bubble" is that a crash usually means that the stock market fell sharply due to some combination of economic conditions. The bursting of a bubble means that what had been called stock market growth was just the formation of a bubble, in the sense that there was no real justification for the growth other than sheer greed pushing up prices irrationally. It is frankly hard to distinguish between the two, and one might say that when you personally are active in the market and it falls sharply, that was a crash. But when you are not active in the market and it falls sharply, those idiots who were in the market produced a bubble which, of course, burst.

There have been three notable crashes in the stock market in the previous three-quarters of a century (in another somewhat cynical play on words, crashes prior to the 1900s were generally called "panics"). The most famous are those of October, 1929, and October, 1987, and that of the Nasdaq in March, 2000. We will track these crashes in great detail in this chronology to show exactly what happened, and how. At least in the case of 1929, the actuality is much different than the myth. For example, the famous Black Tuesday in 1929, held out as the day of one of the most terrible crashes in market history, actually turned out to be a one-night stand.

The real crash of the market of that time took place from April of 1930 onward. The terrible crash of 1987 was reversed in a few years, a rebound that actually was the beginning of the longest bull market in history in the 1990s. The Nasdaq crash of 2000, which in some ways was worse than either of the two earlier famous crashes, is still working itself out. However, we're getting a little ahead of ourselves, and we'll save the details for the rest of the book. The key point is that horrible crashes are standard parts of stock market history, and if you want to play the market, you'd better be ready for a crash at some point.

This is also an appropriate point to say that this Chronology is meant to be a reference book giving the history of the NYSE and the Nasdaq in chronological form. It is not intended to provide investment advice. There are literally hundreds, if not thousands, of such books. They all raise the issue of "if he's so smart, why isn't he rich?" in the sense that someone who truly knows how to beat the market ought to be on the beach in Hawaii being served cool drinks by attentive servants. This is not to demean the limited number of books that seriously attempt to explain how the various markets work, but I personally have always told my friends when they ask me for advice that free advice is worth exactly what it costs. So I can only observe that people should buy books telling them how to get rich quick in the stock market with a great deal of skepticism.

However, having made this disclaimer, there is at the end of this Introduction, and in part of the appendix at the end of the book, some advice about investing in stocks that hopefully will remove the blinding mystique that stocks have for many people. In fact, you *can* get rich in the stock market and many people have. But if you invest for the long term for your retirement as almost all advisors recommend, you can do equally well in many cases by buying a kind of bond that will give you the same return over 20 to 30 years with no risk. For many people, this may be a suitable alternative to investing in the stock market, which can be dangerous to the uninformed. The bond is as free of risk as investments can be, and is an effective alternative to stocks when you want to be sure your full retirement funds will be there when you need them.

Part of the mystery of the stock market are the many stock market indexes that are discussed by the brokers and advisors who deal with stocks. There are in fact a large number of indexes, and they all attempt to provide an indication as to where the market has been in the past, which way the market is going now, and which way it may go in the future. But in a manner analogous to the treatment of the stock market as a whole, there are really only two indexes that need to be covered by this book. The first is the Dow Jones industrials index, which was developed 1896 by Charles Dow, and is still going strong today. The second is the Nasdaq index, which was born in 1971 and is the mantra for anyone looking for huge growth in the market. It has lost a little sheen due to the crash of 2000, but if you listen to a network news show, you will hear the results for the day of at least two indexes: the Dow Jones, and the Nasdaq.

If the news show you are listening to has enough time, they may add the results for the S&P 500, and the Russell 2000, for example. This book will focus on the milestones for the Dow Jones and the Nasdaq indexes, because they truly reflect the history of the top markets in the world. But because there is so much interest in the subject of indexes, the appendix lists all of the other top indexes and describes how they were developed and how they are typically used.

The appendix also discusses the various kinds of investment risks for any kind of financial product we wish to buy and provides specific examples of how a fixed income investment will grow by as much as 20 times if it is held for the proper number of years. All of these investments can be guaranteed by the federal government. The appendix then discusses instances where stock markets have dropped for periods as long as 25 years, which means that anyone near retirement age who is being told to buy stocks for their retirement should think twice about accepting such advice. After outlining methods of evaluating stocks, which can be used to buy stocks on a responsible basis, the appendix describes the "dot.com" phenomenon of the 1990s and discusses how the blame can be widely spread for the collapse of the Nasdaq index and the pain delivered to many investors as a result. Finally, the appendix lists some useful stock market axioms.

To finish this Introduction, let's discuss the mystique issue. Many people have the perception that there is something magical in the stock market. Stocks have a certain aura about them and most people perceive that the only market in which you can have your investments grow by as many as fifteen times or more is the stock market. Actually, as I will show in a minute, any financial product sold in the market will increase by fifteen times or more given enough time and a stable marketplace to support it. So before I outline the chronological history of the market, I want to remove, if I can, some of the aura that stocks have in the market, so that their history can be clearly seen.

After the trauma of the Kennedy assassination in 1963, the market regained its footing and events seemed to return to normal early in 1964. In February 1964, the market hit a new high of 800. This also was a time when I personally became active in the market, and learned a number of lessons. As an example, let's assume an investor was able to buy one "unit" of the market for $800 in early February of 1964. We'll compare the growth of that market unit to a bond that was bought on the first day of January, 1964. This investment was made in the type of bond that does not pay out cash as it goes, but rather permits the investment to accumulate with time (this is called a zero-coupon bond, about which much more will be said in the appendix). We'll assume a yearly interest rate of 8 percent for this fixed investment. It will give us a benchmark against which we can measure the magic progress of our $800 invested in the stock market.

The 1960s were called the go-go years in terms of market growth, and in the 1970s the brokers were pushing the "nifty fifty," as stocks that could be held forever and would grow forever. But of course, they did not. When we reached the new decade of the 1980s, by April of that year, our stock unit had grown from $800 to, well, $800. Sixteen years had gone by and nothing had happened. The market had surged above 1,000 in between, but it surged right back down again. When we compared the return on our fixed investment to our stock investment, we found that the dull fixed investment had grown nearly to $3,000, while our stock return was nothing. A bit of a surprise.

But good things began to happen in the 1980s, and by the summer of 1987, the stock market had climbed above the 2,700 mark. However, in the "crash" of 1987, the market lost a record 22.6 percent in one day (it's still a record percentage drop for one day). The market was back in the high teens. Finally, when the 1990s arrived, the fantastic returns promised from the stock market were delivered in spades. The market went up and up and up, passing milestones of 5,000, 6,000, 7,000 and 8,000 in a two year period between 1995 and 1997.

Then we arrived in January of 2000 at the doorstep of the new millennium. In that month, the market hit its all time high of 11,723. This was an increase of almost fifteen times from the $800 "unit" we bought back in 1964. The market had delivered as promised. But it turns out that the fixed investment account at the same time had grown to almost $12,900, an increase of over 16 times. Moreover, as this is being written late in 2001, the market still has not surpassed its record high of 11,723, and our fixed account is well on its way to $15,000 when the new year of 2002 dawns.

This cautionary tale is not meant to convince you that investing in stocks is a bad idea. But I hope that I have convinced you that, given enough time, a fixed investment account can also increase by 15 or 20 times in value (with little or no risk). Stocks are just another way to invest, not the only way that will give you multiple increases in value over time.

Another point to note is that the fixed account was never less than the value we invested, and every day it was higher than the day before. However, our stock account had spent sixteen years going nowhere. If you had retired in 1964 and counted on stocks to provide your retirement income, you may well have no longer been with us when they struggled back to their original value. Remember, we're talking about current times. It took 25 years for stocks to recover their 1929 value. But that is often dismissed as being in the "old times" that have no relevance to today. However, the period of no net growth from 1964 to 1980 is certainly "relevant" to today.

Perhaps even more relevant is the fact that the Tokyo stock market, at the end of 1989, peaked just under 39,000. Japan was the top economic player of the time, and everyone commented on how the Japanese were ready to replace their Western counterparts. An investment in the Japanese stock market in 1989 was considered the best thing available. By June of 1995, the Japanese stock market was down to 15,000, a drop of 62 percent. Today it has fallen below 12,000, a drop of 70 percent. Anyone retiring in 1989 with the Tokyo stock market as their major investment had an unhappy retirement.

Now that I have gotten your attention, I should point out that if you buy stocks that pay dividends, your financial return will be better than simply the measurement of the value of the market at different times. However, one of the "new" philosophies of the 1990s was to ignore dividends and buy stocks based on their potential to appreciate (such as the dot.com stocks). If you buy those kinds of stocks, the numbers we've being going through are directly applicable.

I want to emphasize that I'm not saying stocks are a bad investment. If you buy fundamentally sound companies and hold their stocks for long periods of time, you will get good returns. But the same thing can be said of fixed income investments of the kind I am talking about. There is nothing magical about stocks. They are not the only way you can get large returns. And depending on your age, you need to be very careful about stock investments, because if they turn down just when you need them, you may not be able to recover.

The essence of achieving large returns in any investment is permitting enough time for the magic of compound interest to take place. In the example I used above, when our fixed investment reaches the $15,000 mark just after the end of 2001, the investment will consist of our original $800 plus

$14,200 in interest. This shows perhaps more clearly than anything else I could say how important time and the "magic" of compound interest is in achieving high returns.

The stock market we are discussing in this book is a wonderful market to find investments of the type that will fit your needs based on your income level and your age. What you need is a stable market that is intelligently regulated by the government, and that is backed by the cumulative huge resources of the many investment companies involved in it. This is the stock market you fortunately have in the United States. But the first rule is still buyer beware.

CHRONOLOGY OF
THE STOCK MARKET

As discussed in the Introduction, the chronology of the stock market in the United States is initially the chronology of the New York Stock Market (NYSE) from the colonial days through 1971. Then the chronology follows both the NYSE and the Nasdaq stock market from 1971 onward. Although many other financial products have been, and are, offered by what most people call the "stock" market, we will focus on the activities concerning the processing of stocks in this chronology. Even those who buy the other kinds of financial products available still think of themselves as buying on the "stock market."

Many people also use the term "stock market" interchangeably with the term "Wall Street," even though for much of the history of the NYSE the stock exchange was located on Broad Street, a few yards around the corner from Wall Street. It wasn't until 1922 that the NYSE had a permanent building entrance actually on Wall Street (11 Wall Street), with nearly all the trading floors being located on Broad Street (as they still are). The Nasdaq has no trading floor at all, but is purely an electronic exchange. Its "trading floor" consists of thousands of computer screens. But the terms "Stock Market" and "Wall Street" are embedded in the language, and there they shall remain regardless of the actual activity pursued in whatever physical location.

This chronology will focus on early trading and the evolution of the stock exchange, the establishment of various market indexes, the development of the regulation of the markets, how the market was affected by certain historical events, and, yes, even the milestones of the famous index developed by Charles Dow, who with Eddie Jones as his partner, founded the Dow Jones company and its baby, *The Wall Street Journal*, in the last quarter of the 19th century. Recommendations about investing occur briefly only in the Introduction and Appendix. This is not a book about how to "play" the stock market. Infamous financial dealers are mentioned only in passing, although the chronology ends with some detail about how the Nasdaq crash of 2000 came about, and how some investment analysts may have contributed to its downfall. Again, the book is intended to be mainly about the market, not those who misused it. To begin at the beginning:

April 4, 1644— The Dutch, who 20 years earlier in 1624 had founded New Netherland in what is now the New York area, and then founded New Amsterdam in 1626 when Peter Minuit made his famous deal to buy Manhattan island for $24 worth of trinkets, started work on a fence at the southern end of what is now Manhattan, to help protect its citizens against raids by Indians (who perhaps now realized they had been had in the deal with Minuit). In an unintended consequence, the fence forced the local cows to establish a path home at an angle to the fence, and this path will one day be known as Broad Street. The fence becomes a fortified stockade wall in 1653 to provide protection against the British, who are once again at war with the Netherlands.

September 8, 1664— Repeating a common historical mistake, the Dutch had long assumed the British will attack by land. But on this date the British attacked by sea and seized both New Netherland and New Amsterdam. The combined area was named after the Duke of York. New York was born.

November 10, 1674— After the Dutch recaptured the colony in 1673, they ceded it back to Britain on this date as part of one of many settlements between the warring nations. The British were back to stay. The wall built in 1653 had since been burned and destroyed, but in 1685 surveyors laid out a street on its prior pathway. Wall Street was born. In 1704, property on Wall Street was ceded to build New York City Hall. It became the setting for George Washington's inaugural in 1789, with New York serving as the capital of the United States.

January 14, 1790— Alexander Hamilton, the first Secretary of the Treasury, proposed that to establish good financial credibility in the world, the United States needed to redeem the "Continentals" (paper money and script the Continental Congress had issued to finance the Revolutionary War). He also proposed that the debts of the states be assumed by the federal government. Southern states were opposed because many had sold their Continentals at bargain prices to Northern speculators. Also, states such as Virginia, which had paid its debts, objected to the fact that states such as New York, which had not, would be bailed out. Hamilton worked out a deal with Thomas Jefferson to transfer the capital to the south, with a temporary hiatus in Philadelphia, while a new federal city was built on the border of Virginia and Maryland. The support of these three key states got the deal done. The capital moved to Philadelphia by the end of 1790 (for what turned out to be 10 years) and then to the new Washington, D.C. The government issued 80 million dollars in bonds (an immense sum in 1790), and the somewhat informal group of traders and brokers that had developed in the booming port of New York immediately became much more serious about the securities part of their business. The bonds had to be sold, and potential brokers emerged from the woodwork to get a piece of the action. Hamilton's transaction ended with the federal capital in one city, and the center of the financial world in another (New York). It has remained that way ever since (although Franklin Roosevelt and especially Harry Truman would try to put Washington back at the financial center as described later in the book). The deal between Hamilton and Jefferson started the series of events that eventually produced the NYSE.

May 17, 1792— A group of 24 merchant-brokers established a more formal operation for trading securities. The bank of the United States had been formed in 1791, adding to the many bank stocks that were now being sold along with Hamilton's bonds. The pact drawn up by the 24 men was called the "Buttonwood Agreement" because it was supposedly signed under a large buttonwood (sycamore) tree. This pact marked the beginning of the New York Stock Exchange. The tree was unique in that the British had burned most trees as firewood when they occupied New York during the Revolutionary War. But the Wall Street Buttonwood, which was perhaps 500 years old at the time of the signing, lasted until it fell in a storm in 1865 (it stood at what is now 68 Wall Street). It was a suitably tough symbol of the eventually powerful exchange founded under its limbs.

June 18, 1812— Congress officially declared war with Britain on this date. The war caused many European investors (ironically, mostly British) to back away from investments in the States, especially after the British set fire to the White House and Capitol building in the new city of Washington in August, 1814 (leading to a series of battles that produced the writing of the *Star Spangled Banner*). But the British had their problems with

Napoleon and unstable kings, and a peace treaty was signed just before the end of 1814. The major impact of the war on the financial markets was that the government's efforts to sell bonds to finance the war showed that an improved financial market was needed in the United States.

March 8, 1817—As a result of the turmoil caused by the war, the traders who had signed the Buttonwood Agreement joined with others to establish a formal organization, the New York Stock & Exchange Board (NYS&EB), which rented rooms at 40 Wall Street. They established a constitution, agreed to meet at regular hours, set minimum commissions, and elected a president and other officers (in 1863 their name would become the New York Stock Exchange).

The 1817 name reflected the parlance of the day. The "board" simply meant a place where brokers associated and provided facilities to buy and sell "securities." At the time Hamilton's bonds were being sold, the word "stock" was simply a generic term for all sorts of securities, and early securities holders in the States generally bought them as an investment to be held for a lifetime. Trading at first was a small activity compared to the marketing of new securities.

The word "exchange" referred initially to the buying and selling of foreign currencies, including the Spanish dollar, which was legal tender in the States until 1857. The Spanish milled dollar (or piece of eight) could easily be divided into pieces as small as an eight with hammer and chisel. Accounts included these fractions, and this is why securities in the States were quoted in eighths. The practice did not stop until "decimal pricing" arrived in 2000 and 2001.

October 26, 1825—The opening of the Erie Canal offers shippers another gateway to the Great Lakes region. It increases the prosperity of the New York area, and New York State bonds to finance the canal increase the trading activity on the Exchange. Ironically, also in 1825, John Stevens of Hoboken, New Jersey, built and operated the first experimental steam locomotive in the United States. I say "ironically" because in the same year the Erie Canal opened successfully, the end of that canal, and all such canals, was signaled by the successful operation of the steam locomotive by Stevens. Railroads spread rapidly everywhere after 1825.

The first railroad stock to be traded on the Exchange was the Mohawk and Hudson, a small line offering service over the 17 miles between Albany and Schenectady (later to become part of the gigantic New York Central). The stock was traded during 1830, the same year the Baltimore and Ohio Railroad began operation. When the Tom Thumb, the first fully operational steam locomotive produced in the United States (for the Baltimore and Ohio) was built, a railroad boom was launched that dominated trading on the Exchange from the 1840s through the 1890s. The railroads soon rendered the Erie Canal (and others like it) obsolete. The railroad boom would drive the physical and economic growth of the United States for the next 70 years, just like railroad bonds and stocks would drive the trading activity on the stock exchange.

May 24, 1844 — The famous first telegraph message ("what hath God wrought") is sent by Samuel Morse. The telegraph greatly improves communication between New York and the brokers and investors outside the city. Previously, a private semaphore service had been established between New York and Philadelphia, with agents stationed on the tops of tall buildings and hills every six or eight miles. Using telescopes to read the flag signals, each agent then sent the news onward. It took only 30 minutes, but the telegraph soon took over.

August 24, 1857 — The Ohio Trust and Life Company failed, triggering the so-called Panic of 1857. It proved to be the final act of Jacob Little, a broker often called the first great speculator. The NYS&EB had been trying to bring more order (and honesty) to the dealings taking place in the financial markets, and in 1853, it strengthened its listing standards. It required companies listed on its board to state the number of outstanding shares and its total capital resources. But speculators had begun their rise in spite of such adjustments.

Little had been the dominant personality on Wall Street for nearly 25 years, making and losing several fortunes. He was known for selling short, a process in which stocks are sold on the market by someone who doesn't own them, but can deliver them later (180 to 360 days later when Little started, but only 60 days later when the rules were changed as a result of his activities). The seller hopes the price will drop by the time he has to deliver, and often he helps the price drop by spreading rumors about the demise of the company, or short-selling on such a scale that lower prices become a self-fulfilling prophecy. It is a process ripe for fraud.

Little was known as the "Great Bear of Wall Street," because the Bear was the symbol of traders who want lower prices (as opposed to Bulls who want prices to go up). These names were established in Europe a century before Wall Street got started. They may have derived from the old practice of Bull-baiting and Bear-baiting with packs of dogs, with the resulting frenzy considered similar to what goes on in stock markets. Also, the bull had been worshipped in several ancient societies because the bull, who could impregnate all of the cows in a herd, became associated with growth and fertility. Thus it has been speculated that the bull naturally became the symbol of growth in stock markets. The Bear, however, was associated with selling short because of the old proverb that says "don't sell the bearskin before the bear is caught." Security traders selling short were called "bear skin jobbers."

But Little was actually a victim in 1857. The discovery of gold in California in 1848 produced a boom in small banks in the next 10 years as $500 million worth of gold was produced. In time they were issuing bank notes without due diligence, and even insurance companies caught the fever. Thus, when the Ohio Life and Trust Company in Cincinnati failed on August 24, 1857, the insurance companies in New York, which was the nation's center for life insurance, went to the banks to draw cash. By October 18 New York banks suspended payment of the dubious notes mentioned above, and 20,000 people lost their jobs. Little lost his last fortune. Other brokers fell also, but by the end of the year the panic was over.

August 16, 1858 — The first message was sent over the trans-Atlantic cable laid by Cyrus Field. He made five attempts to lay the cable in 1857-58, and the first message finally came over successfully on August 16, 1858. However, the cable failed only three weeks later. Field then successfully raised new funds and redesigned the process. In 1866, he successfully laid a cable that represented the initiation of instantaneous communication between New York and London.

As it usually goes with new technology, the success of the cable ended an unique business venture by a Mr. D. H. Craig of Boston, who in the 1850s used Nova Scotia as a place to board steamers bound for the States. He read the latest European newspapers on the ship, then sent the significant news to Boston via carrier pigeons he had brought on board with him. His subscribers thus got the news days before it would otherwise be available. The insatiable desire for information in real time was the driving force behind nearly all the technical advances during the 19th century.

April 12, 1861 — The beginning of the Civil War meant that the securities of the seceding states were suspended from trading. Otherwise the war had little effect on trading in New York. The federal government had to raise capital for the war effort, and some individual states in the north also raised money to defend themselves. Railroads kept booming, and except for the South, the nation boomed right along with them, both in terms of opening new markets to companies, and in terms of the new jobs created by the need to build and operate railroads and acquire the necessary equipment (by the end of the century a single railroad company might have 30,000 employees). The South was devastated by the war, but the rest of the country surged ahead, and the stock exchange did the same.

January 29, 1863 — The NYS&EB changed its name to the New York Stock Exchange (NYSE). "Exchange" had come to mean stock rather than currency exchange, but "board" still informally meant a place where such trading is done. The NYSE ultimately became the "Big Board."

December 9, 1865 — The NYSE moved to its first permanent home at 10-12 Broad Street, just around the corner from Wall Street. The corner of Wall and Broad streets became the center of securities trading in the United States, but the name "Wall Street" continued in popular use, as is the case today. The new building did at least have a narrow arm on the north side with an entrance at 13 Wall Street.

November 15, 1867 — Dr. S.S. Laws, who had been both a gold broker and physics student at Princeton University, modified a telegraph which could impress electrical impulses on a moving tape, probably giving him the credit of being the first to develop the "ticker tape." However, his machine was very cumbersome and costly to operate. Later in the year, Edward A. Calahan, who had become a telegraph operator after the telegraph was invented in 1844, invented a similar machine that used an electric motor to receive the tape. This motor had a ticking sound, and Calahan's development was thus logically called a "stock ticker." Calahan actually should receive the credit for developing the first stock ticker, because his system did work as advertised.

The system developed earlier by Dr. Laws frequently broke down, and Laws himself was not able to supply maintenance people who could repair the system. A young inventor by the name of Thomas A. Edison, who was just starting out in life, was able to make the Laws system work. Laws, of course, gave him a job, and Edison later invented an electromagnetic stock ticker. Edison went on to use his profits from the sale of the company that made this ticker to open his famous Menlo Park laboratory. The rest is history.

Calahan's ticker had replaced a series of messengers on Wall Street who raced around the district delivering news about prices to the brokers who employed them. One messenger had the nickname of the "American Deer" in honor of his great speed. But he couldn't keep up with the ticker. He was yet another who lost his job to advancing technology. In 20 years there would be over 1,000 tickers running in brokerage offices in Manhattan, all fed from the Exchange floor.

October 23, 1868 — A rule was passed permitting members to sell their "seats" on the Exchange. Originally, members actually were given assigned seats when they joined the Exchange. They stopped using chairs of any sort when continuous trading started in 1871, but being a member of the Exchange has continued to be called "having a seat" on the Exchange. When memberships were set at a fixed number in 1868, permitting members to sell their seats was a potential profitable option. But the buyer still had to pass muster by the Membership Department before becoming a member.

February 1, 1869 — The NYSE now required all listed companies to register their securities in an attempt to prevent over-issuance of stocks (also known as "watering" of stocks). However, as will be noted in several of the following items, this attempt, among others, to reduce fraud in the marketplace would be an uphill battle.

May 8, 1869 — Trading volume increased greatly during the 1860s, thanks to the general prosperity and the technical advances making it easier to trade. Other brokerages sprang up in Manhattan to challenge the NYSE. One was called the Coal Hole because of its dingy basement location. It split when members most interested in trading gold went off to form the New York Gold Exchange. Most of the rest of the membership formed the Open Board of Stock Brokers. With less strict rules than the NYSE, it became a key challenger. Also, some members of the NYSE founded a Government Bond Department.

But the NYSE once again achieved domination among the exchanges by merging with the Open Board and the Government Bond Department on May 8, 1869. NYSE membership doubled to 1,060. A new constitution to reflect the mergers was adopted then, and is still in force today.

September 24, 1869 — Jay Gould's attempt to corner the gold market ended in another "Black Friday" on September 24, 1869. Gould went as far as bribing President Grant's brother-in-law and the assistant treasurer of the United States to help in the plot. These two told President Grant not to sell gold (which would depress the market price of the gold Gould and his partner Jim Fisk were accumulating). To keep Grant quiet as the key day arrived, his brother-in-law, Abel Corbin, got Grant to visit a relative in a small Pennsylvania town that had no telegraph service. Grant was to ride there in a private car provided by one of Gould's railroads.

But Grant finally caught on that the parade of people urging him not to sell gold were up to no good. Grant sent a letter to Corbin telling him to stop whatever plot he was involved in. When Gould saw the letter, he decided on September 22 to double cross his partner Fisk before word got out. In a comic opera scene Gould's brokers were running around selling gold on the same trading floors where Fisk was still buying to corner the market. Gould told his agents to avoid Fisk at all costs. The whole business came crashing down on Friday the 24th when Grant announced the treasury would sell gold the next day. The price of gold collapsed, brokers and others found themselves bankrupt, and Gould had to be saved from a mob intent on lynching him. He escaped literally out the back door of his office under the protection of deputies. This was the atmosphere created by the "robber barons" of the "Gilded Age" (see 9/18/1873).

September 18, 1873—Jay Cooke & Company failed (in Philadelphia) due to his excess speculation in railroad stocks. This started a chain reaction that produced the nationwide panic of 1873, and when Cooke closed down, the NYSE closed as well through September 29, 1873. Cooke was one of a number of speculators who rose to power during the 1860s as the ongoing boom of the railroads and the need to finance the Civil War created opportunities to skim off the top (or slurp from the bottom depending on your point of view). Names like Jay Gould, Jim Fisk, (see 9/24/1869), Jay Cooke, Cornelius Vanderbilt, and Daniel Drew became infamous. They were not members of the NYSE, but they were financiers who controlled companies, and bribed politicians to help them manipulate stocks. The period was satirized by Mark Twain in his 1873 novel titled *The Gilded Age*. But, as usual, the truth was even stranger than fiction.

As the 1870s moved on, stocks began to outnumber bonds for the first time in the marketplace. The heaviest trading was still in railroad stocks, followed closely by railroad bonds. Ironically, as the NYSE was making it easier and easier to trade, outside speculators increased their efforts to cheat the general public. Of course, sheer greed made the general public easy to fleece. Some things never change.

December 1, 1873—Trading hours on the NYSE were set at 10 A.M. to 3 P.M. Monday to Friday, with Saturdays set at 10 A.M. to noon. This was part of substantial changes that were made by the NYSE to go to what became known as "continuous trading." Until 1871, brokers met twice daily in morning and afternoon sessions to make bids for stocks as the names of the listed stocks were called from the rostrum by the President of the Exchange. The bids were recorded by the Secretary, and all brokers had to settle their accounts per the list of bids recorded by the Secretary. Following the afternoon session, the news of the key events of the day were announced publicly. However, increasing volume made this practice too unwieldy, and, in 1871, the NYSE renovated its trading floor to support continuous trading. This was a major change in trading stocks. Iron poles with the names of various stocks were installed on the floor, and brokers left their seats both literally and figuratively to walk around the floor to trade at various stations. The change in trading hours was part of this process.

The new system soon gave rise to "specialists," where brokers who traded in one particular stock or type of stock gravitated to one part of the floor and could always be found there. They helped bring liquidity and stability to the market for their specialty by buying for their own account when necessary to keep an orderly market going. According to legend, the first specialist was a member who broke his leg in an accident and had to limit himself to one spot on the floor. The practice quickly grew without the need to break any limbs.

November 13, 1878— Two years after Alexander Graham Bell conducted successful tests in Boston of his new invention called the Telephone, the NYSE installed its first telephones on the trading floor. Within a few years many brokers were linked to the Exchange by phone, and by 1903, when the Exchange opened its new building, 500 telephones were installed around the trading floor.

The telephone was the crown jewel of the key technical innovations of the 1800s (the telegraph, the trans-Atlantic cable, the stock ticker, and, finally, the telephone). These changes in technology supported the mergers and changes in practices (such as continuous trading) that enabled the stock market to handle the greatly increased volume with relative ease. The stage was set for the NYSE to become the top Exchange in the world, as well as the States, early in the next century (replacing London).

Driven by the need to handle this ever increasing volume of trading, the following year, in 1879, the NYSE acquired properties adjoining its present building on both sides so that it could expand. It sold 40 new memberships (bringing the total number of NYSE members to 1,100) to finance the renovations. When the building was finished in 1881, the NYSE had a trading floor measuring 138 feet long by 63 feet wide. It also had an annunciator board at one end to page members. The NYSE was ready for the continuing changes to come.

November 15, 1882— In November 1882 (the actual date is unknown because the company kept no formal records until 1900), Charles Dow and Eddie Jones formed a company to supply financial news, the business in which they were both employed before they decided to start their own company. It would be called Dow, Jones & Company (or most often, simply Dow Jones). They had a third partner, Charles Bergstresser, but all agreed that adding Bergstresser to the company name offended the ear, and they left the name of the company at Dow Jones.

July 3, 1884— In the Customer's Afternoon Letter compiled by Dow Jones, a two-page sheet of the daily financial news (which would grow into the *Wall Street Journal* in five years), the average closing prices of 11 "active" stocks was published. This was the first index of American stocks to be published (other indexes may have been created earlier, but none were published). It was generally considered the creation of Charles Dow, and it was, of course, the first step in creating the famous Dow Jones industrial averages. Dow was simply looking for a way to keep a convenient track of historical trends in the market, and he claimed no special advantage in being able to "forecast" the market.

The first list contained nine railroad stocks (railroad stocks and bonds were the prime movers of the market), and two industrial stocks. The mixed list quickly added another railroad stock, and then evolved as different combinations were tried. But Dow was one of the earliest analysts to see the role industrial stocks would play in the future of the country, and in addition to evaluating railroad stocks, he was looking for a meaningful index consisting of industrial stocks only. Industrials were new, and thus speculative because they had limited past results to use for comparison. Dow continued his quest for 12 more years.

For the record, the initial list published on July 3, 1884 consisted of Chicago & North Western, D.L.& W, Lake Shore, New York Central, St. Paul, Northern Pacific pfd., Union Pacific, Missouri Pacific, Louisville & Nashville, Pacific Mail, and Western Union (the last two being the industrials).

December 15, 1886— The NYSE had its first million share day with 1,200,000 shares traded (111 years later it would have its first billion share day). It was no coincidence that this big day came only eight years after the first telephones were installed on the exchange floor. Also, by 1886, the Commercial Telegram Company, organized in 1882, had over 800 stock tickers operating in New York, Philadelphia, Boston and Chicago. The huge surge in available information drove trading on the NYSE to an ongoing succession of new highs (the wires carrying this information became so thick overhead in New York that the city passed a law in 1884 requiring them to be buried). This apparently insatiable thirst for information supported the initially shaky company Dow and Jones had founded.

March 12, 1888— The infamous "blizzard of '88" dumped 22 inches of snow and enormous drifts on New York City. Only 61 of the exchange's 1,100 members made it in to work, and the exchange closed at noon. Many telephone and telegraph lines were damaged, causing the city to step up its efforts to put the lines underground, as it decreed in 1884. The devastation in March was followed by a celebration later in the year, when the first documented ticker-tape parade took place during President Grover Cleveland's reelection campaign. Only a "veritable blizzard" took place in the fall, but the honor of being the first person to be the object of a ticker-tape parade did not help Cleveland, who lost the election to Benjamin Harrison.

July 8, 1889— *The Wall Street Journal* made its first appearance, as Dow Jones continued to prosper (at least to the extent needed to buy new presses). In the hundred years that followed the founding of Dow Jones and its baby, "the *Wall Street Journal*," the paper that started as a summary of financial news would add general news and become the newspaper with the largest daily circulation in the United States (a position it still held as the next century ended). It would also add international editions that would make it "must" reading among businessmen around the world. In every possible way, the *Wall Street Journal* was an incredible success story.

January 23, 1895— To assist in the distribution of information available about stocks, the NYSE recommended that all listed companies create annual reports that included income statements and balance sheets, and that they distribute these to their stockholders. The formal "Annual Report" was on its way to becoming a fixture.

May 26, 1896— Charles Dow, after 12 years of development, published a stock average consisting only of industrial stocks. It listed 12 stocks, but Dow still must not have been satisfied because the list was published only occasionally in the next four months. The 12 stocks included American Cotton Oil, American Sugar, American Tobacco, Chicago Gas, Distilling & Cattle Feeding, General Electric, Laclede Gas, National Lead, North American, Tenn. Coal & Iron, U.S. Leather pfd., and U.S. Rubber.

October 7, 1896— Continuous publication of Charles Dow's list of 12 industrial stocks begins on this day. Dow also set his separate list of railroad stocks at 20 on October 26 (before that he had a separate list of 20 stocks containing 18 railroad stocks and two industrials), but October 7 is generally accepted as the day that both the Dow Jones industrial and railroad stock averages had their inception. The industrial average was expanded to 20 stocks in 1916, and to 30 in 1928. It has remained at 30 ever since, although the individual stocks keep changing. The 20 railroad stocks were renamed the transportation average on the first day of 1970, but there has been no change in the number of stocks in this average since 1896. Thus, when a utilities average with 15 stocks was started in 1929, the Dow Jones averages consisted of an industrial average with 30 stocks, a railroad (later transportation) average with 20 stocks, and a utilities average with 15 stocks. The overall average had a total of 65 stocks (30 plus 20 plus 15). The count has not changed since.

It should be noted that any reference today to "How's the Dow?" almost invariably means "How's the Dow industrial average?" Many non-professional traders are not even aware there are three Dow Jones averages, and would not wish to know the value of the other averages even if they were told about them. The great strength of the Dow Jones industrials is that they are a historical record. Everyone who dips their toe into the stock market knows the value the Dow Jones industrials had on that fateful first day of stock ownership. There are many better (or at least broader or more specific) market indexes, but the Dow Jones average maintains its historical advantage at the top of the list.

Incidentally, the Dow Jones industrials reached their all-time low in the first year they were first published. They were just below 28.5 on August 8, but this was before their official continuous publishing date of October 7, 1896. They "opened" at 35.3 on October 7, and except for a few days below 35 before the end of the year, it generally has been onward and upward since, though it dipped as low as 41.2 by July 1932.

January 9, 1899— Unaware of the ultimately historical launches it had made in the form of the *Wall Street Journal* and the Dow Jones averages, the Dow Jones company stumbled into troubled times. On this date, Eddie Jones announced he was leaving Dow Jones and the company was being dissolved. The replacement company, however, would continue under the name of Dow Jones, and would be owned by Charles Dow, Charles Bergstresser, Thomas Woodlock, and Frank Brady. Eddie Jones was joining a firm in the industry about which he had been such an avid reporter. No further news about the change was reported. As noted, Dow Jones kept no formal records as a company until 1900. Dow Jones was not in any way a famous name at the time, and all three of the original partners were rather private men. When Dow died four years later at the end of 1902, other newspapers gave his death only two brief paragraphs. Similarly, Jones got only one paragraph when he died in 1920, and Bergstresser got only a brief notice when he died in 1923. Each man could believe he died in relative obscurity. The founders of the original Dow Jones company were somewhat like the famous painters who died destitute and unknown only to have their paintings command millions of dollars amid much renown in the future.

April 21, 1899— A "Review and Outlook" column, written by Charles Dow, first appeared in the *Wall Street Journal*. In ongoing columns he attempted to educate readers in the stock and bond markets as he saw them. These columns became the basis for future writers to sell books and newsletters about the "Dow Theory" although Dow himself never claimed to have such a theory. A book published in 1922, *The Stock Market Barometer* by

William Hamilton, went through seven-editions and established the "Dow Theory" industry. Hamilton at least was a true contemporary of Dow. Hamilton joined the *Wall Street Journal* in 1899 and eventually became the editor of the editorial pages. He stated that the Dow Theory was "fundamentally simple," and then took about 300 pages to explain it. But people eager to believe there was a "secret" to the market that could make them rich couldn't get enough of the book. Such books are still published today (as it often goes, Charles Dow has yet to see his first royalty check from books about "his" theory).

March 3, 1901— The already legendary J.P. Morgan Sr. announced plans for what would become the U.S. Steel Corporation, in a megadeal made possible by the sale of the Carnegie Steel Corporation by Andrew Carnegie to Morgan. Carnegie then retired to work on distributing his fortune (he made over $300 million on the sale to Morgan). Morgan assembled several other companies and merged them together as U.S. Steel, which he then sold to the public for $1.4 billion, making U.S. Steel the first American corporation capitalized at more than $1 billion.

April 30, 1901— The NYSE moved to temporary quarters at the Produce Exchange on the same day that trading volume reached 3 million shares for the first time. Both of these events were specifically related, because the NYSE had decided to build a new building on the site of its old building to handle the ever increasing trading volume (which grew even more as the public scrambled to get a piece of the new U.S. Steel Corporation). The temporary quarters for the NYSE permitted the plans for its new building, which were completed earlier in 1901, to be implemented. The new building clearly would be a palace of security trading. It was reasonably easy to decide that the additional business necessary to support a new palace would be achieved because stock trading had tripled just between 1896 and 1899, and would double again by 1901. The huge increase in volume was a good thing because, as is usually the case, the budget for the new building was "only" $1 million, while the final cost came in at $4 million. Among many other new technical advances, the new palace was one of the first buildings in the world to employ air conditioning.

May 9, 1901— As yet another example of the frantic activities driving up trading volume in 1901, Northern Pacific Railroad (NPRR) stock reached $1,000 per share on this date, after selling at $96 in late April. Railroad baron E.H. Harriman was battling with James Hill and the famous J.P. Morgan Sr. for control of the railroad.

At first, Harriman was succeeding because Hill and Morgan were unaware of the amount of NPRR stock Harriman was quietly buying. When

Hill discovered the plot, he was unable to reach Morgan, because Morgan, as was his habit, was visiting a lovely new countess in France and had left word that he didn't wish to be disturbed. When Morgan was finally disengaged from his latest affair, he marshaled his forces to begin buying NPRR stock to prevent Harriman from gaining control. Wall Street bears, who had been happily selling the stock as it went up, expecting to realize huge profits when they replaced their borrowed stock at lower prices sometime in the future, panicked when they realized there was no stock left at any price to replace their short sales. Twice before, in 1873 and 1884, people speculating in NPRR stock were ruined by short sellers. This time, it was the short sellers who were being ruined. The stock price jumped to $1,000 per share exactly because the short sellers had been trying to buy the stock at any price to cover their short positions. Most other stocks fell sharply in response to the anticipated fallout from the NPRR debacle, and, for a few days, at least on the books of lending banks, many Wall Street brokers were technically insolvent. The stocks they had pledged as collateral for their Northern Pacific short sales were also collapsing. It was the typical result of an overheated bidding war.

Morgan, Hill, and Harriman finally came to an agreement and permitted the short sellers of Northern Pacific to cover their positions at $150 a share, thus avoiding the collapse of many of the brokers on the Street. Of course, the members of the general public, who didn't fully understand what was happening, responded to the scent of quick profits with buy orders, and lost huge sums when the stock fell back. Their greed notwithstanding, the "small traders" pleaded for government intervention. Although nothing happened at the time, this was one step in the process that led to the creation of the Federal Reserve system in 1913, when the government camel finally got its nose under the tent.

As an aside, Charles Dow had written an editorial in the *Wall Street Journal* in 1899 commenting that he was afraid that the market was ceasing to be "professional." He saw this as a negative development because he thought that the general public tended to take profits in one group of stocks and then run immediately to another group trying for another quick profit. This was not the basic purpose of the stock market. The disasters of 1929 and 2001 were due to a large extent to the problem that Dow foresaw in 1899. Once again, the more things change, the more they stay the same.

September 9, 1901— The cornerstone for the NYSE's new building was laid on this date at 4:30 in the afternoon. One of the most complex problems involved in the construction of the new building was that the intention was to erect a new building on the same site as the old building and the property that had been acquired immediately to the north and south of the old building. This meant that the foundation of the old building had to be removed before the new building could be constructed. A new 776 ton vault was built beneath the old building. When the new vault was ready, the securities from the old vault were transferred downward to the new vault, and the old vault was blasted away. This was sort of an in-place test for the new vault, which it passed with flying colors.

March 13, 1902— Charles Dow resigned as director and president of the Dow Jones Company. Already in poor health, Dow would die a little over eight months later on 12/4/1902 at the age of 51, due to an apparent heart attack. In addition to his resignation, he announced that he had found a buyer for his stock. Since Dow held the majority of the stock, if he sold the stock after he resigned, that would mean the Dow Jones company would have a new owner. This is exactly what happened.

Clarence Walker Barron, owner of the Boston News Bureau which published in Boston items similar to what Dow Jones published in New York, was to take over the company with his wife, Mrs. Jessie Waldon Barron. The background of the Barrons is a little hazy, as Barron had been a boarder with Mrs. Barron in Boston for fourteen years before they married in 1900. Mrs. Barron would hold nearly 90 percent of the Dow Jones stock in her name, and she would become a very active member of the board representing her husband. On 3/31/1902 the stock transfers were made and the Dow Jones company was now under new ownership.

As noted in the entry for 1/9/1899, the Dow Jones company was not well known at all when all of the original founders died, and they never got to realize how famous the company and its publications would become. However, in all fairness, credit must be given to those who came next (even after the Barrons were gone) and built the Dow Jones company and the industrials index to a colossus in the financial reporting business.

April 22, 1903— Opening ceremonies for the new NYSE building were held. The building was occupied for the first time on the following day, and many sources list April 23 as the completion of the building; but it was actually complete the day before. The building took two years to complete, rather than the one year that was scheduled. However late it was, the new building was a huge success.

It's hard to imagine nearly a century later the impact the new NYSE building had on the city of New York. It was a magnificent building, and its opening was like the opening of a new museum or cathedral. In years to come, especially during the crash of 1929 and the crash of 1987, huge crowds gathered outside, feeling the need to be where, to many of them, very mysterious but important things were taking place. It would become an icon of the city, and tourists would come to see it in growing numbers.

The trading floor of the new NYSE was directly behind six Corinthian columns facing Broad Street. It had marble walls, a gilt ceiling 72 feet high, and giant windows on the east and west sides, each of which measured 96 feet wide by 50 feet high, and weighed 13 tons.

More than 20,000 people toured the building at the opening ceremonies. By the end of the century, the NYSE was one of the most popular tourist sites in New York City, attracting nearly half a million visitors every year. In 1922, a 23-story tower was built next to the new building to accommodate the ever growing trading volume. This new building was also a marvel of engineering for its time. The new trading room was on the first floor attached to the main trading room in the main building. As "simply" an addition, the new trading floor was nicknamed "the garage." Perhaps the most significant fact of the new 23-story tower was that it was built exactly on the corner of Broad and Wall streets, and thus the Exchange once more could claim to be located on Wall Street. It adopted 11 Wall Street as its official address from that time onward. But the picture most people carry around in their minds when they think of the NYSE are the massive columns on Broad Street.*

June 21, 1904—On this date, the NYSE was presented with a gift from the Imperial Russian Government. It was a stone and silver urn crafted by Carl Fabergé. It was a token of appreciation to the NYSE from Czar Nicholas II for listing the Imperial Russian Loan in 1902. The exquisite urn still stands in the corner of the boardroom of the Exchange today.

But although the urn still exists, the Russian government, following the Bolshevik Revolution in October 1917, defaulted on the bonds. They were finally suspended from trading on the NYSE in 1921.

January 12, 1906—The Dow Jones industrial average reached 100 for the first time. It would stay high during most of 1906, but it lost 45 percent of its value by the end of 1907. Essentially, the loss was both due to, and a cause of, the 1907 panic near the end of 1907.

October 22, 1907—On this date, the Knickerbocker Trust Bank of New York collapsed. This was later identified as the trigger for the so-called Panic of 1907, but the panic was actually due to a number of problems during the year. The stage was set for it when the stock market began to fall on

---

The 1992 book The New York Stock Exchange, the First 200 Years, *produced by the NYSE, is the source for most of the above facts. I strongly recommend it to anyone interested in the history of the Exchange, and I wish to express my debt to this book as a key reference source.*

3/13/1907 in response to a decline in general economic conditions. As the market continued to slide over the next six months, bankers began to have problems because many depositors were unsure of the security of their deposits. In mid-October, the Mercantile National Bank in New York, which had become overextended due to some improper speculative investments, closed.

The Knickerbocker Trust Bank was next on the critical list because it had invested heavily in the United Copper Company, and the bank became shaky when United Copper shares fell sharply. In another case of truth being stranger than fiction, the directors of the Knickerbocker Bank, gathering in the upstairs room of a restaurant on the night of 10/21/1907, thoughtlessly left the door ajar as they discussed their problems. While they were trying to decide whether or not to open the bank for business the next morning, eavesdroppers heard the conversation and spread the word. By daybreak on 10/22/1907, thousands of depositors were lining up at the bank's main office to withdraw their money. The Knickerbocker exhausted its resources of $8 million in a little over two hours and closed its doors shortly after noon. Not all of the depositors were able to get all of their money, and several weeks later, prompted by the suicide of Charles Barney, president of the bank, some of them committed suicide as well.

J.P. Morgan Sr., who was semi-retired and attending a religious retreat in Richmond, VA, had already been called on October 17 and had agreed to come to New York. Morgan made no move to try to resuscitate the Knickerbocker, because an audit showed that its situation was hopeless. But Morgan got a pledge from Treasury Secretary George B. Cortelyou to put $25 million of government money at Morgan's disposal. With the $25 million in his kitty, Morgan was able to convince several other New York banks to form a separate pool of money to help in a rescue effort. He identified the Trust Company of America as the next bank most likely to fail, but one which he thought could be saved. Morgan then pumped money into the Trust Company bank and other banks, which were now growing shaky up and down the East Coast. The banks were trying to slow the outflow by paying the depositors in small change, while counting it three or four times. Any trick that would gain time was tried.

The panic spread to the stock market as banks began calling in their margin loans, and stock prices continued downward, which in turn triggered more margin calls. On Thursday, 10/24/1907, NYSE president Ransom H. Thomas told Morgan that they needed another $25 million immediately or more than 50 brokerage firms might fail. Morgan, with assistance from John D. Rockefeller, who made a deposit of $10 million in the Union Trust Bank, told Thomas not to close the Exchange until its usual closing time of exactly 3:00 (Thomas was getting ready to close it ahead of time). Morgan collected a batch of bankers at his office at 2:00, got Rockefeller to agree another to another $5 million, and then called the roll of bankers to pledge enough money to save the Exchange. They came up with $27 million to keep the Exchange open. Morgan sent word to the trading floor that the money would be available and, sitting in his office across the street from the Exchange, he could hear the muffled cheers of the brokers across the street.

This was not the end of the crisis. On Saturday, 11/2/1907, several banks still looked like they might fail when the weekend ended. Morgan summoned the city's leading bankers to his mansion on 5th Avenue and locked them in the library. He presented a rescue plan requiring additional cash (his firm signed up for its share), and then sat silently in the corner playing solitaire while the bankers debated his plan. Morgan said the doors to the library would remain locked until an agreement was reached. The bankers argued through the night, but finally agreed to provide the money. The panic soon ended.

Although Morgan was portrayed in the press as a savior, many in Congress, who sat by and did nothing in the crisis, complained that it was all a plot by the banks to ultimately make money. It was criticism of this type that would finally lead to the establishment of the Federal Reserve System in 1913, the same year J.P. Morgan died.

December 23, 1913— The Federal Reserve Act, which created the Federal Reserve Board and its 12 Federal Reserve Districts, was signed into law by President Woodrow Wilson. J.P. Morgan's last public appearances were at the hearings held by Arsene P. Pujo, Chairman of the House Committee on Banking and Currency, to determine if such an act was needed. The hearings were very contentious, as Pujo was accused of ignoring the habeas corpus act and forcing many bankers (including Morgan) to testify. The hearings concluded that there was a great need for a Federal Reserve system, which the *Wall Street Journal* and many others had already concluded as far back as the Panic of 1893.

The Pujo Hearings were soon forgotten, but the act was passed by Congress and signed by Wilson just before the end of 1913. It was charged that several of the proposed 12 Federal Reserve Districts had been gerrymandered in accordance with the desire of certain politicians. But this was certainly nothing new in Congress. The Federal Reserve System was much needed, but, as the *Wall Street Journal* stated after it had been adopted, it required "wise administration" to achieve its goals. In the first real crisis in which the Federal Reserve System would be tested, the crash of 1929, it failed absolutely due to "unwise" administration, to put it as mildly as possible.

July 31, 1914— The NYSE closed from this date through 12/11/1914 due to the start of World War I. The assassination of Austrian Archduke Franz Ferdinand on 6/28/1914 triggered a complicated system of alliances which resulted in the European countries declaring war on each other during the month of July. As the incessant threats of war became real, various countries around the world began closing their exchanges. The last major exchange to close was the one in London on the morning of July 31. When news reached the NYSE that they were the last major exchange open in the world, the Governing Committee met just before the scheduled 10 A.M. opening to decide whether or not to open the doors. The NYSE voted not to open until further notice, and they remained closed through 12/11/1914, even though President Wilson declared on August 4 that the United States would remain neutral. When the Exchange finally did open on 12/12/1914, certain minimum price restrictions applied. The price restrictions were removed on 4/1/1915, when the NYSE was finally officially open for business.

October 13, 1915— The NYSE changed the basis of quoting and trading in stocks from a percentage of par value to dollars. This did not change any fundamental fact of trading on the floor, but in retrospect, it would make it much easier for the public to get more involved in trading since having quotes and stock values in dollars made them much easier to understand.

April 6, 1917— The United States declared war with Germany and its allies after a series of events following Germany's declaration of unrestricted submarine warfare on 1/31/1917. As has always been the case, the major effect on the NYSE was to help raise the funds necessary for the conduct of the war. For the first time, the NYSE as an exchange endorsed a particular security — Liberty Bonds. Between 1917 and 1919, over $23 billion would be raised in four Liberty Bond drives and one Victory Loan drive. The sale of these bonds was so successful that a separate ticker tape system was set up to process the bonds.

October 22, 1917— A huge Liberty Bond rally was held on the floor of the NYSE. The annunciator board was converted to a billboard urging people to buy bonds. Ironically, these bonds represented the first taste of "investing" for many people and would later form the basis of the public participation in the booming market of the 1920s. This result, as it turned out, may not have necessarily been for the best.

November 11, 1918— The Armistice ending WWI was declared on this date, following the announcement of a "false armistice" four days earlier. The NYSE closed for the day and a huge ticker tape parade was held. Since that date, a moment of silence has been observed on the trading floor every November 11 at 11 A.M. (the "Eleventh hour of the eleventh day of the eleventh month.")

A major practical result of the armistice was the fact that the NYSE now became the basic financial center for the rest of the world. This was especially true because the British Treasury imposed an embargo on foreign loans to keep much-needed British currency in the country. The result was that London gave up its historic role of financing world trade, and in the years to come, everyone in the world would turn to Wall Street when they needed to raise capital. This turn of events was helped by the fact that during the war, huge amounts of gold were sent to New York for safekeeping, if not in payment for guns and supplies. The movement of gold to the west started slowly in 1915, and then became a torrent. In the month of March 1916, the United States imported almost as much gold in that single month as it had in any previous entire year. Without a doubt, when the war ended, the United States was number one financially.

January 2, 1920— The Dow average, now based on 20 different stocks since September 1916, opened a new decade on the first trading day of the new year just below 109. The average had spent most of the war trading between 50 and 100, generally on the higher side of that range, but it closed 1920 at 72. The great bull market of the 1920s had yet to begin.

April 26, 1920— The Stock Clearing Corporation was established by the NYSE. A similar Clearing Corporation was established in 1892 to centralize and expedite the transfer of securities from broker to broker. The Corporation established in 1920 was to centralize the delivery and clearing of securities among members, banks, and trust companies. In every way, the NYSE was getting bigger and more influential.

September 16, 1920— As noon approached on September 26, a driver pulled an old horse-drawn wagon up to the curb on Wall Street just a few yards east of Broad. This was the corner on which the building housing J.P. Morgan and Company sat. The driver got out and disappeared into the normal milling noontime crowd, and moments later, the wagon erupted with a huge explosion. It turned out that the wagon was packed with explosives and 500 pounds of broken-up window sash weights. The blast shattered nearly every window near the corner and severely damaged the J.P. Morgan building and the U.S. Assay office on the opposite side of the street. A total of 30 people were killed and more than 100 injured in the explosion, which left deep scars in the facade of the Morgan building. These scars intentionally have never been removed and remain clearly visible today. The person or persons responsible for this crime have never been found. It was widely assumed that the bombing was the work of anarchists, and it actually triggered a period of almost a decade during which people of "questionable" heritage were rounded up and questioned.

One note about the explosion is that at the time the wagon was pulling up to the corner of Wall and Broad streets, almost a billion dollars in gold was being moved under armed guard from the old repository in the sub-Treasury building to a new repository in the Assay Office next door. Just before the explosion, the porters of the gold and their guards had quit for lunch and moved into their respective buildings, closing the well-barred side entrances after them. Not only did it save their lives, it probably prevented the spectacular raid on the U.S. Treasury that would have happened if a significant portion of that gold had been destroyed. This would have caused a worldwide financial crisis, but it is not clear that the bombers knew about the movement of the gold or intended this result.

In the investigation that followed the explosion, it was found that in April, 1919, bombs had been sent to a number of prominent people. These bombs were intended to explode when the packages were opened. Most of the bombs failed to reach their destination because they were delayed in the New York City Post Office, and then discovered, because they had insufficient postage.

December 31, 1923— The Dow closed the year at 96 after beginning the year at 99. Many experts have identified 1923 as the year the great bull market of the 1920s started; but as is often the case, carefully reading the Dow closings does not show what the "experts" claim. During the year, the Dow did, however, often poke its head above 100. Trading volume kept growing, driven primarily by huge growth in the automobile business (led by General Motors).

July 31, 1926— Morgan partner Thomas Cochran consented to a Saturday midnight interview with a ship news reporter just before going to bed on the liner *Olympic*, which was scheduled to depart early the next morning. On Monday morning, the Dow Jones financial news ticker carried the interview. The key item was that Cochran was reported as saying that, in essence, General Motors was cheap at its present price, and should go at least 100 points higher. Many readers of the interview were shocked because members of the prestigious Morgan Company rarely gave advice about stocks, let alone made a price prediction. Within minutes of reading the tape, brokers and traders on the NYSE floor were clustered about the post where GM was traded. By the end of the day, more than 250,000 shares of the stock had been traded, and its price went up from 189½ to 201. Virtually the same thing happened the next day. On Wednesday, Cochran, now a thousand miles at sea, claimed he had not authorized any statement predicting the price of the stock. Otherwise, he stood by the interview. *The Wall Street Journal* praised Cochran for his frankness, as everyone discounted Cochran's claim of not predicting the price. They knew he was just saving face with Morgan. The tip was a good one, because GM announced a 50 percent stock dividend on August 12. It was obvious that something new was happening in the market, because one of the oldest companies was pumping up stocks with price predictions and the *Wall Street Journal* was praising the company accordingly. This new acceptance of "hot tips" from brokers fueled the growth of the market, and the extent to which the general public was becoming involved. It may have seemed like a good idea at the time, but in three years, it would seem like a very bad idea.

December 31, 1926— The Dow closed at 157 after starting the year at 159. The averages stayed relatively high all year, and a constant upward movement was clearly evident. The NYSE tightened its listing rules during the year, but speculative fever was building anyway.

July 27, 1927— At a time when great concern was being expressed at the volume of stocks being bought on margin, and the Wall Street credit structure was becoming overextended, on this date the Federal Reserve voted to lower the discount rate from 4 to 3.5 percent. The Federal Reserve had been created in 1913 precisely to address this type of problem, but at a time when it was clear credit needed to be tightened, it was eased instead. Many experts feel that this single idiotic act had more to do with the 1929 crash than any other single act.

The basic problem with buying stocks on margin is that any market dip is greatly exaggerated. If you buy a stock selling for $100 a share on 90 percent margin (a common margin at the time) it means that you put up $10 and the broker puts up $90. If the stock goes up $10 a share, you will have made a profit of $10 on your $10 investment, or a return of 100 percent. If you borrow the initial $10 from someone else, as many people did, your profit is infinite. At any rate, you are doing the "proper" thing: making money for yourself using other people's money.

However, if the stock goes down $10, your broker will immediately call you to send him more money because he has loaned you $90 and all he has for collateral is a stock worth exactly $90. If you cannot send him the money right away, he then sells your stock to get his $90. In a falling market, selling your stock causes it to drop even further. In addition, if the person who loaned you $10 asks for it back, you have no way to get it. And now he has to sell some stock to get the money he needs. The market goes down even further. The net result is, that in all schemes of this type, everything is fine as long as the market goes up. When the market goes down, disaster can result.

The job of the Federal Reserve is to adjust credit up or down as needed to control margin buying. In a situation where a market disaster was just waiting to happen, the Federal Reserve did exactly the wrong thing. Broker loans shot up to $4.4 from $3.3 billion during the course of the year, an unprecedented increase. President Coolidge said that he did not consider the increase in broker loans big enough to cause any unfavorable comment. Even Wall Street could not believe its ears. The public assumed that Coolidge's comment indicated approval of margin buying. For once, "Silent Cal" really should have remained silent.

The Federal Reserve at the time was driven by its leader, Benjamin Strong, who was far more concerned with international politics than with what was happening in the country. He saw lower interest rates as helpful to Europe's economy, and that's what he was trying to achieve. When he later became ill, the Federal Reserve regained its senses, but it was too late.

November 17, 1927 — President Coolidge stated that America was "entering upon a new era of prosperity." He meant it in the sense that the old cycle of boom and bust was over, and steady growth in the wealth and savings of the people would continue, along with continuously raising stock prices. Again, people essentially felt that if the President tells you things are going to continue to boom, it must be true. The stage was being set for the coming bust.

December 31, 1927 — The Dow closed the year above 202, after breaking the 200 barrier on December 18. It began the year at 155. The gain was a result of the incredible decision of the Federal Reserve to lower the discount rate. Speculative fever was now running higher than ever, although it must be noted that most experts felt that only about 1.5 million people, among a population of 125 million, were involved in the market. However, this figure does not include institutional investors and banks, which accounted for the bulk of the trading. No one knows how much of this trading involved individual investors.

June 13, 1928 — The *New York Times* announced on this date that Wall Street's bull market collapsed on June 12, with a "detonation heard 'round the world." Actually, the Dow dropped only seven points between June 9 and June 12, and it gained it all back on June 13. Clearly, people were very nervous. It must also be pointed out that a drop of seven points in 1928 corresponds to a drop of about 350 points now for a Dow average near 10,000, where it stands as this is written. As we follow the crash in October of 1929, we will point out how apparently small drops in the Dow were actually very significant for the averages of that time. Many people who have become accustomed to drops of several hundred points in the Dow today have a hard time understanding why a drop of seven or 10 points in the 1920s was seen as a market "break."

Rather than collapsing as stated in the *Times*, the market soared to 20 percent above its low point in June, and by November it was 50 percent higher. The Senate Banking and Currency Committee held hearings on the question of brokers' loans in February and March 1928, but nothing happened to curtail the loans. Even the Federal Reserve Board, now that Benjamin Strong was no longer a factor, raised the discount rate from 3.5 to 5 percent in three steps during the year. But in spite of this action, stocks surged in the second half of 1928, and over that six month period, broker loans increased by another $1.5 billion, more than they had increased in the whole year of 1927.

The NYSE opened a new and expanded trading room to handle the increased volume in 1928 (trading volume increased nearly five-fold during the decade). There were some signs that some people were beginning to worry about the degree of speculation. One of them was Joseph P. Kennedy (father of the future President, Jack Kennedy) who had moved his family from Boston to New York to take part in the opportunities on Wall Street. He began to liquidate many of his positions in 1928, feeling that the market rally could not be sustained. There is a legend that Kennedy was given a stock tip by either an elevator operator or a shoeshine stand operator as he walked into his office building, and he decided that if people at this level were giving stock tips, speculation had gone too far, and it was time to get out of the market. Kennedy later claimed he made up the story to defuse the resentment that losers in the market would feel at his success. No one knows which, if either, of these stories is true. But it is true that Kennedy got out of the market with his fortune intact before the market crashed.

December 31, 1928— The Dow closed the year at exactly 300, 50 percent higher than the near 200 at which it had begun the year, and 50 percent higher than the little murmur in June the *Times* had gotten so excited about. The bull market ignored the three rate increases by the Federal Reserve during 1928, and any other sense of restraint, for that matter. The big bust of 1929 was one step closer.

February 2, 1929— On this date early in 1929, the Federal Reserve (the "Fed") decided to resort to another kind of action. This was triggered by the fact that in January 1929, the Dow rose by over 10 points (equivalent to an increase of nearly 350 points for a Dow at 10,000), and broker loans went up another $260 million. It was finally clear to the Fed that either the actions they were taking were ineffective, or nobody was paying attention to them any longer, or both. The Fed attempted to use what could be called "moral suasion," but it should have known that this market was not likely to react to that kind of action. It stated that the Federal Reserve system no longer intended to use its resources for the creation or extension of speculative credit. However, speculation went ahead as usual, but the comment did have the effect of slowing the money supply, and on March 26, a crisis was reached in the resources available to fund a broker's call for more margin. At this point, Charles E. Mitchell, president of the National City Bank of New York, undercut the Fed by offering cheap money. The little crisis ended, and speculation went on.

Mitchell was just the most current example of how New York bankers at the time were breaking the rules of law and ethics to keep the market boom going. Mitchell, and others like him, were making several hundred thousand dollars a year in salary as presidents of their banks, a real fortune at that time. But in spite of this, they didn't hesitate to violate the trust they held to try to make more. Mitchell and others like him were penalized after their practices came out in government hearings after the crash. But at the time, they showed no restraint and did everything they could to draw more players in to support the market rise and their questionable associated activities. If the most significant single event in causing the crash was the poor performance of the Fed, the single key emotion that helped to cause the crash was greed.

But regardless of what was going on behind the scenes, everyone did continue to come into the market, and volume continued to soar. To handle this volume, the NYSE added 275 memberships in 1929, to go to a total of 1,375. And they remodeled the trading floor, replacing the old trading posts with larger horseshoe-shaped posts to make trading more efficient.

May 8, 1929— *The Wall Street Journal* for this date carried an editorial severely scolding the Federal Reserve Board for refusing to raise the rediscount rate further (the directors of the New York Federal Reserve Bank also recommended an increase). The Federal Reserve did nothing (later, in his memoirs, in perhaps a classic case of the pot calling the kettle black, at least in terms of who to blame for the worst decisions relative to the crash and the following Depression, President Hoover called the Washington Federal Reserve Board members "mediocrities").

But if the Fed was still paralyzed, some others were not. Following the March dip that was "solved" by Mitchell's offering up more money, some speculators decided things had gone far enough. Along with Joe Kennedy, who had begun to withdraw in 1928, famous names such as Bernard Baruch and John Raskob began to liquidate their positions. Arthur Salomon, head of the famous brokerage bearing his name, also ordered his firm to begin liquidating questionable margin accounts that had been extended to customers. Baruch offered some free advice, stating that "repeatedly in my market operations, I have sold a stock while it was still rising — and that has been one reason why I have held onto my fortune." He also urged bankers to form a pool to support the market in case of a crash, and offered $6 million of his own money as an initial contribution. No one else was interested in contributing. Baruch and other speculators of his class simply began to vote with their feet. They were getting out.

May 25, 1929 — General Motors, which at the time was looked on as a serious competitor to the legendary Henry Ford, but not yet the huge company it would become in the 1950s, reported record profits of over $61 million during the quarter ending 3/31/1929. Much credit for this was given to John Raskob, the former stenographer for Pierre du Pont, who induced the du Pont company to buy control of General Motors and put Raskob in as a top executive. Raskob (who, after he left GM, later led the effort to build the Empire State Building, which he insisted had to be a few hundred feet higher than its competitors) had introduced the new idea of buying cars on credit, which had become an immediate success. Raskob then moved to Wall Street and became a flaming bull.

Raskob later wrote a famous article published in the *Ladies Home Journal* insisting that everyone ought to be rich, a goal they could accomplish if they followed his careful instructions. At any rate, Raskob was often thought of as the prime symbol of the ever-growing bull market. But even he finally thought things had gone to far, and got out of the market before the September crash. Those who believed they knew more than Baruch and Raskob stayed in for the final ride. It was an exhilarating ride, but it ended badly.

August 9, 1929 — The Fed, in a marvelous example of "too little, too late," raised its interest rate to 6 percent. Again, nobody paid much attention, as the Fed had become at best a figure of fun, if not outright derision. In fact, at the time such business indicators as building starts, consumer spending, wholesale commodity prices, and employment rates had all begun to fall, after steadily rising through June 1929. An interest rate increase was exactly the wrong thing to do in the face of these declines, but nobody was paying much attention to rational actions. For example, broker loans passed $6 billion soon after Labor Day.

September 3, 1929—The Dow hit a record high of 381.2 on this date, to the great joy of the bulls in the market. Of course they couldn't know that the Dow would not come back to the 381 level until the end of 1954— a full 25 years later. The roller coaster was now pointed down its sharpest incline.

September 5, 1929—On September 5, there was a 10 point drop in the Dow averages, which became known as "the Babson break." Roger Babson of Wellesley, Mass., who looked more like a goateed pixie than a financial advisor, told an audience at a New England financial luncheon, "I repeat what I said at this time last year and the year before, that sooner or later a crash is coming, and it may be terrific." He predicted a 60 to 80 point drop in the Dow, and said "factories will be shut down ... men will be thrown out of work ... the vicious cycle will go into full swing, and the result will be a serious depression." It was a frightening forecast (and amazingly accurate), but the key problem was, as Babson said, he had said the same thing last year and the year before. Everybody giggled and moved on.

But the break did have one important effect. The fact that the market did go down from its highs, and not recover fully, was impressive in its own right, and Babson had dared to use the word "crash," which had been entirely taboo. Now the word became widely talked about in Manhattan. The *New York Times* ran a column saying that there were certain frightening parallels between today and 1907, when a panic had risen unexpectedly. In what seems an almost macabre comment in reflection, the paper said that now there was the new force of the Federal Reserve, and that would help stabilize the market. It's hard to say how such a responsible newspaper could be so wrong.

September 30, 1929—The Dow ended the month just above 343. This was a total of 38 points, or 10 percent, below its peak of September 3. In today's terms, a drop of 10 percent would be over 1,000 points. This was a large drop for just one month, and a lot of the decline happened just in the last 10 days. The signs were indeed ominous.

October 14, 1929—On this date Professor Irving Fisher of Yale, a highly regarded economist of the time, made what became one of the most ridiculed statements of the century. Fisher, in a speech at a meeting associated with an investment group, said that "stocks have reached a permanently high plateau," and that he expected the stock market to go "a great deal higher than it is today within a few months." After the crash, Fisher was widely ridiculed and held up as an example of the crazy rhetoric that helped cause the market to crash.

The sad part of the story is that Fisher was not a nut but a careful student of the stock market. He believed that stocks had great growth potential, especially stocks of small and medium sized companies. He was sure these stocks would outperform those of the larger companies. His analysis was exactly correct, but he was living in the wrong decade.

Fisher put his money where his mouth was. He had accumulated more than $10 million (about $100 million today), and he kept buying stocks right through the crash. Following the axiom about not fighting the market would have helped him greatly, especially since he was still buying on margin, probably his worst sin. As his losses mounted and margin calls kept coming, he was forced to borrow from his wife's sister, who had a sizeable inheritance. He finally sold his house back to Yale University and rented it back from them. Nothing kept him afloat. He and his wife moved to a small apartment, and when his wife died her sister cut his loan interest to one percent, but he still could not make the payments.

Fisher died in 1947, just one more victim of the crash of 1929. But I have included his history here because one could say he was much more a victim of his own arrogance than the crash. If he had stopped fighting the market, and waited to apply his investment ideas sometime after the market hit its low in the middle of 1932, he might have died a rich man. But he was also another example of the fact that one can easily pass on while waiting for the market to come back (remember, it took 25 years for the market to come back to its 1929 peak).

October 16, 1929 — On this date the New York Investment Bankers Association stated that most issues of "public service stocks" were selling far above their intrinsic value. *The Wall Street Journal* criticized the association, saying it should be more careful in its generalizing, and declaring that the report was already outdated when it was issued. Also, Charles Mitchell, the unethical banker who was leaving Germany on an ocean liner, had said a few days earlier, "I see no reason for the end-of-the-year slump some are predicting. The markets generally are now in a healthy condition." The Dow had nothing to say, but it was now down to 336, another seven point drop since the end of September, and it was still headed down.

October 21, 1929 — On this date, Monday, October 21, the big artillery was finally put into action. William Hamilton, editor of the *Wall Street Journal*'s editorial page and of *Barron's Magazine* (and author of the book *The Stock Market Barometer* in 1922 pushing the Dow Theory — see entry for 4/21/1899) published an editorial in *Barron's* stating in essence that the Dow Theory was indicating a possible bear market. Hamilton also inferred that although the warning signs were definitely present, he did not expect the speculating and investing public to pay much attention to them. Unfortunately, he was right on both counts.

The warning was enough to cause a drop in the market to a low of 315 on this date (Monday the 21st). But traders could not believe anything bad could really happen to them, and when the market bounced back up to 321 at the end of the day, only three points below the close on the previous market day (Saturday, October 19), everything seemed fine. However, the frantic movement up and down on October 21 produced a volume of just over six million shares, the third biggest volume in the history of the NYSE. The infamous Professor Fisher stated that the drop was only "a shaking out of the lunatic fringe that attempts to speculate on margin." On the next day, Tuesday, October 22, Charles E. Mitchell arrived home from Europe and said simply that "the decline has gone too far," and that "the patient was fundamentally sound."

October 23, 1929— The Dow got up to a high of 330 on this date, following a recovery of six points to 327 on the previous day, Tuesday the 22nd. This back-to-back increase was a good sign. But after hitting its peak of 330 today, the Dow plunged to 306 at the close. This was a loss of 6.3 percent (630 points in today's terms). The Dow lost a record 20.6 points in just the last hour of the day, and the tickers ran nearly two hours late. It was noted that both Paris and London also suffered big declines. The coming debacle was not going to be limited to just New York. Brokers made margin calls well into the night, and this action hung over the market when it opened the next day.

October 24, 1929— The time for talk was over. On what would become known as "Black Thursday," a new record of almost 13 million shares were traded (the previous record was just over 8 million), and in the parlance of nearly everyone who writes about this event, "prices fell sharply." Actually, on this day, the Dow closed only six points below its close of the previous day. It was the fact that the Dow fell 34 points during the morning that was so significant (this was a drop of about 11 percent, or 1,100 points in today's terms). The low was reached in less than two hours of non-stop selling at record volumes after the opening. It was this unprecedented morning selloff that earned the name "Black Thursday."

What brought the Dow back from its opening slide was a replay of the 1907 panic, where J.P. Morgan had ridden to the rescue (see entry for 10/22/1907). Morgan himself was long since departed from the scene, but near noon on Black Thursday, several bankers had gathered in offices of his surviving company, which was still located across the street from the NYSE. Also attending the meeting was Richard Whitney, the vice president of the

Exchange, who was acting as president because the president of the Exchange was in Hawaii on an extended honeymoon. The market immediately began to recover when word of the meeting spread. It was expected that action would be forthcoming.

Whitney started the action at 1:30. With a consortium of pooled money behind him, he marched directly to the trading post where U.S. Steel was traded and placed perhaps the most famous order in NYSE history. He bid 205 for 10,000 shares (205 was the price of the previous sale), and then went around the trading floor placing similar orders for other stocks. In a few minutes he had placed orders for more than $20 million worth of stocks. The brokers cheered as he proceeded around the floor, and everyone understood the symbolism of his actions (later in the year, trading post number two, where Whitney made his bid for U.S. Steel, was "retired" from the trading floor and presented to Whitney, who kept it on display outside his office). The panic stopped for the day, and by the close, the market had retraced its steps under heavy volume. The Dow ended its day not far below where it had closed the previous day. The main result of "Black Thursday" was that lights burned into the morning hours as Exchange workers struggled to process the day's paperwork.

October 25, 1929 — Friday morning newspaper headlines read "Richard Whitney Halts Stock Panic." On both today and Saturday the Dow closed near its Thursday afternoon closing level. It appeared the stock market had dodged a bullet. Everyone was glad to echo the claim by Thomas Lamont, head of Morgan, who had said on Thursday, after the meeting of the bankers, that "there has been a little distress selling ... caused by a technical condition of the market." President Hoover added "the fundamental business of the country ... is on a sound and prosperous basis." Denial had moved in next to greed.

It is interesting that so many prominent people kept reassuring the public. In today's perhaps more cynical world, people have learned that when the President or other high officials insist that there is absolutely nothing to worry about, it's time to worry. It is possible that in those days people were more trusting of statements from their leaders, but I doubt it.

At any rate, Whitney was the hero of the moment. He became president of the NYSE from 1930 through 1935, and he also became the spokesman for Wall Street both in Washington and the nation at large. He would steadfastly deny that anything was wrong with the operation of the market. What only a few knew at the time was that Whitney was hopelessly in debt to the tune of about $2 million due to ill-chosen speculative ventures in the Florida land boom and other companies. Only the forbearance of his brother George and the Morgan Company prevented his bankruptcy, but Whitney continued to live on a grand style and continued speculating. In his personal life he was the epitome of denial. When he finally turned to embezzlement to cover his losses, he ended up in Sing Sing prison in 1938. Sentenced to five to ten years, he was paroled in 1941 and lived in obscurity until he died 33 years later in 1974. The 1966 novel by Louis Auchincloss, *The Embezzler*, was based on Whitney's story.

October 27, 1929 — Sunday was a day of relative calm since the NYSE was closed as usual.

October 28, 1929 — Monday, October 28 was actually the day of the "big crash." Nearly every reference says Tuesday, October 29 ("Black Tuesday") was the day of the *really* big crash. But the crash on Monday the 28th had the largest percentage loss in history at the time (12.82 percent) and is still the second biggest such loss in Dow history, trailing only the 22.61 percent loss the market suffered nearly 58 years later on October 19, 1987. The volume on Monday the 28th was over 9 million shares, the second biggest in history to that point, behind Black Thursday. But where Black Thursday was truly only the day on which someone rained on the stock market's parade, Monday the 28th and Tuesday the 29th were the days in which a full scale deluge hit the market. Monday made it perfectly clear that something unprecedented was now happening in the stock market, regardless of the comforting words from the nation's leaders.

October 29, 1929 — According to legend, this is the day of the big crash. The famous headline in *Variety* on Wednesday, October 30 read "Wall Street Lays an Egg." This has helped fix the 29th as the day of the big crash. But actually, on the 29th, the Dow lost "only" 11.73 percent, compared to a loss of 12.82 percent the previous day. However, the volume on the 29th was a then-record 16.4 million shares, which was 78 percent higher than the volume on the 28th. So one could say that there was bigger participation in the crash on the 29th, even if the actual loss was not as large as on the 28th.

Another point to make about the 29th is that the Dow was rallying by the end of the day, and it closed 18 points (or seven percent) above the day's low. That means the Dow was on its way back at the end of the day, and in another little noted effect, it continued upward through the following day.

October 30, 1929 — While *Variety* was running its famous headline, the Dow averages were bouncing back in a major way on Wednesday the 30th. In fact, the Dow's gain on Wednesday the 30th was 12.34 percent, bigger than its loss on Tuesday, and it was the second-greatest percentage gain for the Dow in its history. October 30 still remains in second place, even after all the subsequent monstrous rallies that have taken place in the Dow in the twentieth century.

The reason that many of the Dow's largest gains in history took place in 1929 and the early 1930s was because the Dow was at a relatively low absolute level in those days. But nonetheless, the fact remains that the "huge" losses of "Black Tuesday," October 29, 1929, were almost completely reversed the very next day. What's more, the volume on Wednesday the 30th was almost 11 million shares, bigger at the time than any other day except for Black Tuesday and Black Thursday. So the rally on the 30th had nearly as much support as the "crashes." Hardly anyone remembers the somewhat astounding fact that the "crash" on the 29th was a one-night stand.

November 13, 1929 — On this date, the Dow closed at 198.7, the lowest closing level for the year 1929. This was 48 percent below the peak the Dow hit on September 3. At this point, the $80 billion stocks had been worth in September was now down to $50 billion. But once again, on the next day, November 14, after reaching its yearly low on November 13, the Dow gained 18.6 points, or 9.4 percent. That gain, on November 14, is still the seventh greatest gain percentage in history. The Dow simply would not stay down for the count. From the 14th onward, the Dow continued to move slowly upward. Most accounts say that the market was in a state of disarray after its crash on the 29th, but in fact, the market rebounded sharply after having its big losses and continued growing through the end of the year.

December 31, 1929 — The Dow closed the year at 248.5. Since it closed 1928 at exactly 300, this represents a loss of only 17 percent for the year 1929. It's useful to note that the Dow continued climbing through the spring of 1930.

April 17, 1930 — On this date the Dow reached a peak for 1930 at 294.1. This represents a gain of 48 percent from the November 1929 low. This means that in April 1930, the Dow was back to within 4 percent of its closing value just before the infamous Black Thursday. At this point in April, 1930, the Dow had regained nearly everything it lost in the famous events of 1929. Optimism abounded. In fact, in May, the Secretary of Commerce said that "normal business conditions should be restored in two or three months." The upbeat quote for June came from the secretary of labor, who said, "The worst is over, without a doubt." Then, also in June, President Hoover himself, meeting with a delegation of clergymen who were anxious for a public works program, said, "You have come sixty days too late. The depression is over." The venerable *Wall Street Journal* probably helped the optimistic mood by saying in an editorial on February 10, 1930, that "Based on the well-known Dow Theory ... the stock market has said definitely that the worst of the current industrial recession has passed." As the Dow continued upward to new highs for 1930 in April, it was not unreasonable that the President and his cabinet began to feel very comfortable. The problem was that the worst of the Depression was about to begin at the time all of this optimism was evident.

The point of this discussion is that the "crash" of October 1929 did not "cause" the Depression, nor for that matter, cause many politicians to think there was a problem to address. The April rebound in the Dow showed that the losses in the "crash" had nearly all been regained six months later. The "real" crash took place in the two years after April 1930, following the optimistic comments in Washington. Not until 1954 would the Dow regain the level it reached in April 1930. By July 1932, the Dow would be at 41.2, a loss of 89 percent from its peak of September 1929 (a drop of 66 percent from its high in April 1930). The decade-long depression of the 1930s was due to a number of things, but considered objectively, the spectacular events of October 1929 hardly played a part at all. In fact, as shown, by April they were nearly forgotten, as such things go.

Probably the most notable events caused by the debacle of October 1929 were the changes that took place in the 1930s to restructure the way Wall Street and environs were organized. The losses of October 1929 (and in the years following) completely wiped out enough people, most of whom were playing on margin, to create an atmosphere of revenge. In the early 1930s, people began to look for scapegoats.

April 11, 1932— On this date, Senate hearings began to attempt to find the causes of the stock market plunge. Later taken over by Ferdinand Pecora between the election of Franklin D. Roosevelt in November 1932 and his inauguration in March 1933, the hearings were initially burdened by the fact that President Hoover was sure there was a conspiracy in the way short sales affected the market. As is usually the case when people start looking for conspiracies, there were none to be found. However, Pecora did uncover a large number of bankers who had committed breaches of law and ethics. (See entry for 2/2/1929 regarding Charles E. Mitchell et al.)

As a result of the investigation, Mitchell was forced to resign in February 1933. Albert Wiggin of Chase, who had sold shares of his own company short while he was president of the company, also resigned. He was replaced by Winthrop Aldrich, who was the brother-in-law of John D. Rockefeller Jr., starting the heavy Rockefeller involvement with what became the Chase Manhattan Bank.

As a result of these hearings, people lost what little trust they had left in bankers and accelerated their withdrawal of funds from the banks and their hoarding of cash. Banks began to close nationwide. The international fear that Roosevelt would devalue gold after he took over put pressure on the gold supply in the U.S., which reinforced the collapse of the banks. It was clear that Roosevelt would have to act quickly after he took office in March 1933 to prevent a nationwide collapse of the banks.

March 4, 1933— This was the day of Franklin Roosevelt's inauguration, and the first act of his new administration was to declare a bank "holiday" to stop the ongoing run on the banks. The NYSE also closed on this date due to the holiday, and stayed closed though March 14. Roosevelt also effectively took the U.S. off the gold standard at the same time. Rushing into action, Congress, in exactly eight hours on March 9, passed the Emergency Banking Act, which essentially handed dictatorial powers to Roosevelt. The President made his first "fireside" chat on March 12, and the famous "First 100 Days" of action were under way.

Soon after, the Banking Act of 1933, otherwise known as the Glass/Steagall act, was enacted. It created the Federal Deposit Insurance Corporation (FDIC) to guarantee payments to customers, so that they could be convinced to leave their funds in the banks. It also required that banks select between commercial and investment banking. As a result, J.P. Morgan chose commercial banking and spun off its investment business as Morgan Stanley & Co. Many new investment banks appeared in the years following the Banking Act.

May 27, 1933— Less than 90 days after Roosevelt was inaugurated, the Securities Act of 1933 was approved. Its basic purposes were to provide full disclosure to investors and to prohibit fraud in connection with the sale of securities. Its major vehicle for doing so was to define carefully how new securities had to be registered before they could be offered for sale. The details of the registration process were almost surely lost on the general public, but there was no doubt that they recognized the law was intended to force Wall Street to clean up its act. By now, there was great public approval of anything seen as punishing Wall Street.

June 6, 1934— Just a little over a year later, The Securities Exchange Act of 1934 was enacted. It instituted government regulation of securities trading for the first time, and its most significant step was the establishment of the Securities Exchange Commission (SEC) to oversee Wall Street. It also gave the Federal Reserve Board the authority to regulate margin interest rates.

There was considerable resistance at the NYSE and elsewhere to the establishment of the Securities Exchange Commission. President Roosevelt, in one of his typically clever appointments, made Joseph P. Kennedy the first Securities and Exchange Commissioner. It was hoped this would reduce the resistance of Wall Street to the commission, because Kennedy had been in the trenches as a stock speculator during the 1920s. He had also been smart enough to get out of the market before it crashed. Many critics claimed that Roosevelt was putting the wolf in charge of the sheep, but this kind of appointment was a common technique for the President. There was no doubt that Kennedy knew where the bodies were buried, but it was hoped that he would bend over backwards to accommodate his prior friends on Wall Street.

This hope was realized and Kennedy had a very successful year as chairman of the SEC. He went on to his eventual reward as ambassador to the Court of St. James in England. He was replaced by James Landis and then, in 1937, William Otis Douglas. Douglas would eventually become a very controversial member of the Supreme Court, and he had no end of controversies in his position as chairman of the SEC. But Kennedy had done such a good job in his first year that the commission continued to operate well through the 1930s and afterwards.

January 27, 1938— On this date, a committee headed by Carle C. Conway (known as the Conway Committee) published a report recommending a substantial number of changes to the organization of the NYSE. Douglas was very much in favor of the report, because it gave him everything he wanted (an outside paid president, a technical staff, non-member governors, and provisions that essentially would increase the influence of liberals within the Exchange). But the present president of the Exchange, Charles R. Gay, was also very much in favor of the report, because he knew these changes were needed to bring peace between the NYSE and the government regulators.

In what would become a symbolic victory of the government regulators over the prior influential members of the Exchange, the governing committee of the NYSE board held a vote to decide whether or not to accept the Conway report. The acceptance was unanimous, except for a negative vote by Richard Whitney, the hero of Black Thursday. (See entry for 10/24/1929.) Ironically, it was the last vote Whitney would make as a stock exchange governor. As a result of the changes ordered by the Conway Committee, William McChesney Martin, Jr., was appointed as the Exchange's first full time president at an annual salary of $40,000. Martin in later years would become a chairman of the Federal Reserve.

April 11, 1938— Richard Whitney, as a result of being found guilty of an embezzlement to cover his investment losses (see entry for 10/24/1929), was sentenced to five to ten years in Sing Sing, the infamous prison in New

York state in which most felons served their time. Whitney had vehemently opposed both the New Deal and the Securities Exchange Commission. With the fall of one of the most public proponents of the NYSE, there seemed to be a lessening of the nastiness between government regulators and Wall Street. There was a sense that the "Old Guard" on the Street had died with the imprisonment of Whitney. He was paroled in 1941, and lived in obscurity afterwards (see entry for 10/25/1929).

June 30, 1938— William McChesney Martin Jr. was formally elected president of the NYSE. Around the same time, SEC chairman Douglas said, "The day of the crackdown on Wall Street is over. The prosperity of the Stock Exchange is not incompatible with the national welfare." Douglas was correct in his feeling that the relationship between Washington and Wall Street had improved, but there were still many regulators in Washington thirsting to continue their attacks on Wall Street.

December 31, 1939— The Dow closed the 1930s at 150.2, down almost 100 points (or 40 percent) from the 248.5 at which it closed 1929. The Dow had jumped from its 1932 low of 41.2 up to about 100 following Roosevelt's inauguration in 1933 and his famous "First 100 Days" of action. The Dow hit its peak for the 1930s at 194.4 in March of 1937. But by the end of March 1938, it was back below 100 again. Complaints that Roosevelt had not produced any real change were bubbling to the surface. The economy was still in trouble, and the dip in the Dow reflected this fact. However, the actions of the mad former wallpaper hanger in Berlin, Adolf Hitler, and the threats of war produced by his actions did much more to pull the economy out of its doldrums than any new program Roosevelt could pull out of his hat. The anticipated and actual tooling up to produce weapons improved the economy and brought the Dow back up to 150 at the end of the decade (50 percent above the level it had fallen to in March 1938).

December 7, 1941— The date "that will live in infamy" caused the U.S. to declare war on Japan the next day, and on Germany and Italy on December 11. The NYSE delisted the stocks of the enemy powers, but because Wall Street was still looked upon with suspicion by Washington, that was nearly their only contribution to the war effort. The seven bond drives that paid for World War II were led by the Treasury and supported by the Federal Reserve, which kept interest rates low. The attitude in Washington was best summed up in a statement by President Harry Truman after the war (although Truman had hated Wall Street since the 1930s). Truman stated that he wanted "to keep the financial capital of the United States in Washington. This is where it belongs — but to keep it there is not always an easy task." Truman, at least, wanted no part of the idea that the financial capital was in New York, while the political capital was in Washington. His concept was shared by many New Dealers, who had become used to the idea that only Washington could solve the nation's problems. The fact that the financial capital had been in New York since Hamilton's deal with Jefferson in 1790 (see entry for 1/14/1790) was of no interest to such Washingtonians.

Before and after the attack on Pearl Harbor, the Dow stayed rock solid at 150, and then rose slightly by the end of the month. At least on Wall Street, the sneak attack had not produced any sense of panic.

September 2, 1945—Japan formally surrendered after agreeing to do so on August 14. WW II was officially over. The Dow was running steadily near 175, and the market generally kept rising through the end of the 1940s. But, simply stated, the 1940s were a lousy time to be a stockbroker. It was looked on as a somewhat disreputable occupation, and volume and floor activity were very low. A seat on the Exchange was sold for $17,000 in 1942, the lowest price of the 20th century (buying and holding such a seat would have been an excellent investment, because in 1999, a seat was sold for $2.65 million). The stock market was generally avoided as being simply too speculative, although the Dow average kept climbing slowly upwards after the war. By 1947, there were 25 percent fewer brokers, dealers, and underwriters employed in Manhattan than there had been in 1940.

November 2, 1948—On this date, Harry Truman won his big upset victory over Tom Dewey (in spite of the famous headline in the *Chicago Tribune* announcing Truman's defeat). This was bad news for Wall Street. Truman loved to call the *Wall Street Journal* the Republican's bible while he was on the campaign trail as a way of convincing "the little people" that he was one of them.

Truman had continued his hatred of Wall Street with an anti-trust suit in October 1947 against the "Wall Street 17." The so-called "17" were 17 investment banks that Truman claimed were conspiring to eliminate competition. At this time in the United States, many communist witch hunts were already well underway. Regardless of the "crime" they were accused of, the term "Wall Street 17" was enough to make most people think the bankers were doing some evil communist task. It was good campaign fodder, but after the hearings had dragged on for six years, the case was found to be so weak it was finally thrown out of court and never came to trial (see entry for 10/10/1953). But it had served its campaign purpose by then.

December 31, 1949—The Dow ended the 1940s at 200.13. It had just climbed over 200 for the first time in over three years on December 30.

Since the Dow had closed the 1930s at 150.2 (see entry for 12/31/1939), its close of just over 200 on 12/31/1949 represented a gain of 33 percent for the decade. As the 1940s ended, the economy was good, people were buying, and stock prices were slowly climbing. But Wall Street, with a cloud of the "Wall Street 17" hanging over its head, still suffered from a bad image.

December 26, 1950— *The Wall Street Journal* published for the first time daily changes from the previous close in the Dow Jones stock averages. The changes were shown on a percentage basis, as well as by the number of points. This was intended to make the daily changes in the industrial, transportation, and utility averages directly comparable to each other. But this did not help solve the problem that the general public is usually confused by the word "averages." When they were initially published in 1896 (see entry for 10/7/1896), the Dow Jones averages were exactly that. But as the number of stocks included in the averages changed, and the stocks themselves split their shares, the divisor in the Dow Jones "averages" had to be changed to maintain continuity. This is actually a problem with any stock index, and as Dow Jones insists, the averages are simply a statistical compilation called an average. Like all averages, the number does not reflect individual performances, but only a combined performance of the stocks in the so-called average.

September 29, 1952— On this day, the trading hours were changed to 10 A.M.–3:30 P.M., and Saturday trading was eliminated. Wall Street was starting a massive education plan to go directly to the public, both to improve its image and to attempt to bring more of the "little people" into the market.

January 5, 1953— The New York Curb Exchange officially changed its name to The American Stock Exchange on this date. The New York Curb Exchange had begun informally in the 1790s. Its name was an exact description of the exchange. Brokers stood on the street in the financial district usually dealing in stocks of small companies. Later, they stood near the NYSE so they could look in the NYSE for information and then conduct their own trading in the street. When the telephone was introduced, the curb brokers rented cheap space in nearby buildings (even often using window ledges) so they could communicate with the clerks in the buildings who had access to the telephones. This gave them more rapid interchanges of information. The brokers, both in the buildings and the street, would communicate with each other via a complicated series of hand signals. The brokers on the street (and window ledges) generally were young men who were willing to stand outside in bad weather and conduct their business.

In 1921, the curb market moved indoors into a new building at 86 Trinity Place. But, although you could move the men off the curb, you couldn't move the curb out of the men, and they named their new building The New York Curb Exchange. It remained that way until this date in 1953, when it was renamed the American Stock Exchange. But all that changed was the name inscribed above the entrance to the building.

The American Exchange underwent a major expansion in 1977. But where the NYSE ultimately built new stations in the air and lowered them onto the floor (see entry for 8/18/1982), the American Exchange took advantage of the height of the first floor trading room and built an extra floor above the trading floor.

June 4, 1953— For the first time, NYSE member firms were permitted to incorporate so that they could get easier access to capital. Woodcock, Hess & Company is the first member firm to incorporate.

October 10, 1953— The trading volume on this date was 900,000 shares. This marked the last time that the daily trading volume would be under 1,000,000 shares.

More importantly, during this month Judge Harold Medina dismissed the anti-trust suit that was filed against the "Wall Street 17" in October 1947. Medina fortunately was a man of extremely high integrity, and the only thing he was out to get was the truth. He stated that "I have come to the settled conviction ... that no such combination, conspiracy, and agreement as it is alleged in the complaint ... was ever made, entered into, conceived, constructed, continued, or participated in by these defendants." It was a stinging rebuke to the people who brought the charge, but most of them no longer cared because they had since left the government following the election of Dwight Eisenhower in November 1952. This little-noticed dismissal was a major boon to Wall Street. The government attacks were finally over, and Wall Street could now pay attention to improving its marketplace. A real boom was under way in the United States, due to the pent-up consumer demand due to both World War II and the Korean War (which ended in July 1953).

Thus, October 1953 represents the true beginning of the stock market ride in the second half of the century, which will make the ride in the first half of the century look like the toddler's ride at the fair on the toy choo-choo.

November 23, 1954— On this date the Dow closed at 382.74. This was the first time the Dow had closed over the 381.17 that was the all-time high in September 1929. It took 25 years plus almost three months for the

Dow to get back to its September 1929 level, but in the next few years the Dow would continue to rocket upwards.

In the meantime, the NYSE was undertaking an intensive public relations and advertising campaign to win "the hearts and minds" of the "little people." They started a monthly investment program (MIP) in 1953 to enable small investors to buy stock through regular monthly payments as small as $40 per month. In 1954, they launched an educational and marketing program called "Own Your Share of American Business," aimed directly at expanding participation of the public in the stock market. By the end of the 1950s, the number of individual stockholders in the country would nearly double to 12.5 million. Mutual funds became popular again, and pension plans and institutional buyers began to come into the market. These latter buyers had generally avoided the stock market as being "too speculative."

The stock market, whether deliberately or not, was now singing the favorite American tune. "Moonlight and roses and romance" notwithstanding, the real favorite of Americans is "do you sincerely want to get rich?" In addition, one of the most popular radio show hosts in America, Walter Winchell ("Good evening Mr. and Mrs. America and all the ships at sea…"), began to tout stocks in 1954. His recommendation could not be called professional, but the fact that he was recommending stocks at all showed how much the public mood about Wall Street had changed. Stock brokers could once again enjoy the opportunity to become all-stars.

December 29, 1954— As if to help in the celebration, the Dow went over 400 for the first time, barely one month after it had regained its September 1929 all-time high. The road upward was now clear on the horizon.

March 12, 1956— The Dow went over 500 for the first time on this date.

February 20, 1959— The Dow went over 600 for first time on this date.

December 31, 1959— The Dow closed the 1950s at 679.36, an increase of 3.4 times (or a gain of 240 percent) for the decade. The NYSE was completing planning for an expensive 16 page investment guide for individuals that would be inserted into the *Reader's Digest* in 1960. The NYSE was determined to help the investment boom go on into the 1960s, and by choosing the magazine with the highest circulation in the world (not to mention a highly "middle class" readership) at the time for its insert, it was continuing to reach out to the general public.

May 17, 1961— The Dow continued its inexorable upward climb by going over 700 for the first time on this date. With the market continuing upward, the average daily volume for 1961 would exceed 4 million shares per day. This is nearly three times the level immediately following World War II.

November 22, 1963— On the day John Kennedy was assassinated, the market opened at 733, only 28 points below the all-time high of 761 it had reached a few weeks earlier on October 29, the 34th anniversary of "Black Tuesday." The market was generally continuing to climb.

Immediately following the initial reports from Dallas, the stock market was hit by a wave of selling. The NYSE board of governors assembled and voted to close the market at 2:07 P.M. This was the first time in NYSE history that panic-inducing bad news led to an unscheduled suspension of all activity in the middle of a trading session. The market was essentially in an uproar because more than one third of the day's volume was transacted in the 27 minutes between the first report from Dallas and the closing of the market. The Dow fell "only" 24 points (3 percent), but it was a record decline for such a short time. However, it turned out that the performance of the specialists on the floor was exceptional. They were net purchasers of stock, showing that they were trying to maintain a fair and orderly market. This is the planned function of a specialist, but never before had it worked so well under such trying circumstances. The market closed down approximately 21 points from its close on November 21, but by the time the markets reopened on November 26, they were up 11 points from the closing on the 21st. Essentially the market never missed a beat during the trauma of November 1963.

Unknown to the public, there was another crisis for the NYSE during this time. On Tuesday, November 19, the firm of Ira Haupt & Co. was found to be insolvent. A client of the company was unable to meet nearly $19 million in margin calls in the commodities market. It appeared that over 20,000 customers of the Haupt firm, including many who simply owned stocks on the NYSE, faced the possibility of losing all the securities and cash in their accounts. There was no insurance at that time for broker accounts.

By Friday, when the assassination was announced, it was clear that Haupt's attempts to raise capital were almost certain to fail, and the firm would have to declare bankruptcy. The only good news was that the emergency closing due to the assassination provided time for the NYSE board of governors to address the situation. Since the NYSE was also closed on Monday, November 25, which was a day of national mourning for the President, the board of governors was able to finalize and announce a rescue plan.

When the market reopened on Tuesday, prices immediately rose, as noted above, because the smooth transition of federal power during the crisis impressed everyone. The losses of the previous Friday were erased on

Tuesday, with a volume of 9 million shares, the largest volume of any day in 1963. The rescue of Haupt & Co. took place entirely behind the scenes and led to the establishment of special NYSE trust fund for such emergencies. This finally became the Securities Investor Protection Corporation (SIPC), which was created by Congress in 1970. The SIPC is similar to the FDIC, in the sense that it protects investors in brokerage firms. There is no federal guarantee on the funds, but all stock brokers put up enough money to essentially insure that investors will get their money back, barring a cataclysmic event.

It is ironic that the events leading to the creation of the SIPC, which was a very positive event in the history of the stock market, took place entirely out of sight behind the traumatic events of Kennedy's assassination. Sometimes it's true that when one door closes, another opens.

February 28, 1964— On this date, the Dow closed above 800 for the first time. The market had obviously shaken off the events of November 1963 with ease. But as noted in the Introduction, a long period of flat performance was about to begin. The Dow's performance in the 20th Century can be broken into the following periods:

- From 1900 to 1930, the Dow grew 5.7 times in 30 years.
- From 1930 to 1954, the Dow was flat for 25 years.
- From 1954 to 1964, the Dow grew 2.3 times in 10 years.
- From 1964 to 1980, the Dow was flat for 15 years.
- From 1980 to 2000, the Dow grew 15 times in 20 years.

The Dow bounced up to 1,000 a couple of times between 1964 and 1980, but it fell below 600 in the same period. It is shown as "flat" because at the starting point in 1964, and at the ending point in 1980, it was stuck at 800. The lesson to be learned is that the Dow is a boom or bust process. It always has been, and it always will be. You can make lots of money if you get in at the right time or get out at the right time. Timing really is everything.

January 28, 1965— On this date, the Dow crossed the 900 mark for the first time. It was continuing its spectacular run upward of the 1960s, but in spite of the hope that it would soon pass the magic 1,000 mark, it wouldn't get there until seven years later.

July 14, 1966— The NYSE Composite Index was introduced on this date. The index measures the price trend of every common stock listed on the NYSE. It was calculated continuously, was available from the NYSE's computers, and was periodically flashed over the tickers nationwide. Its advantage, of course, is that it takes into account every single stock. Its disadvantage turns out to be that it takes into account every single stock. Unless there is an event that produces considerable panic, or euphoria, the changes in the index are relatively small. It is commonly quoted in summaries of the performance of the market on a given day, but it does not come close to capturing the imagination of investors in the way that the Dow Jones Index does.

It is claimed that the impetus for the NYSE Composite was a request from President Johnson's White House staff that the Dow Jones company change to the Dow Jones Industrials. President Johnson felt that the Industrials did not accurately represent economic conditions, and he recommended a change that would make the economy look better in terms of the Dow Jones averages. President Johnson had a habit of requesting changes in items he did not like, regardless of the facts of the situation. The president and publisher of the Dow Jones Company, Bill Kerby, said simply, "No." It was not a word President Johnson was fond of.

As a result, so it is claimed, the NYSE started its own market index to please the President. As noted above, the NYSE Composite is a greatly expanded index, and many said it was therefore more representative of the economy. Whatever its merits, it simply is not competitive with the Dow Jones Averages in terms of usage by investors.

As an interesting side note, the NYSE Composite Index was made possible by the fact that the old ticker and quotation system, which used pneumatic tubes, was computerized by the NYSE in 1966. This was, at the time, a dramatic change. It may seem hard to believe today, but until 1963, the Dow Jones averages were calculated by hand by a "little old man" seated in front of his favorite ticker. He recalculated the averages each hour by monitoring the tape for the current prices of the stocks in the average. The Dow Jones company switched to a computer system in 1963, but the limitations of the system meant that the Dow Jones averages were calculated only every half hour. The NYSE Composite, by comparison, was and is calculated continuously. There are many similar changes made in the NYSE during the century that brought the computer into use to replace systems that seemed, at the least, quaint by today's standards.

December 20, 1966 — The transmission of trade and quote data from the trading floor was declared fully automated on this date. The NYSE was doing a good job of using electronics and automation to try to handle the growing paperwork crunch, but many member firms were not able to keep up.

April 1, 1968 — The trading volume reached a record 17.7 million on this date, the first time that the previous all-time high volume of 16.4

million recorded on 9/29/1929 (Black Tuesday) was surpassed. The new volume record quickly became 19.3 million on April 3, and then it rose to 20.4 million on April 10, the first time the volume had crossed the 20 million share mark. This was not a panic in terms of a falling market, because the Dow was running well into the 900s again. The crisis this time was the fact that Wall Street had done much too good a job of selling itself, and by now everyone wanted to get into the market.

In the 1960s alone, golfer Arnold Palmer used the trading floor as a putting green for an NYSE advertisement, and opera singer Roberta Peters and author Irving Stone also did advertisements for the NYSE. In addition, TV newscaster Chet Huntley made an album of three long-playing records in which he had conversations with four investment experts. Going from the perhaps sublime to the ridiculous, or at least the funny, the NYSE produced a series of thirteen five-minute films showing the immensely popular Kukla, Fran and Ollie (Fran was the straight woman for puppeteer Burr Tillstrom, who played the puppets Kukla and Ollie) shilling for Wall Street. Mergers were taking place everywhere and conglomerates were forming in many industries. The 1960s were nicknamed the "go-go" years by Wall Street brokers. This was the good news.

The bad news was that the sheer volume of paperwork generated by all of the new players in the market was putting a terrific strain on many member firms of the NYSE. The NYSE (and other exchanges) had to proclaim "holidays" on otherwise normal business days in an attempt to cope with the mess of record-keeping. The NYSE opened an additional trading room in 1969 to handle the increased activity. It was called the Blue Room, for the very good reason that the walls of the room were blue. But nothing seemed to help. The average daily volume jumped from 3 million shares in 1960 to 6 million shares in 1965, and then 11.6 million by 1970. This is an increase of 400 percent in the decade of the 1960s.

Between 1968 and 1970, between 100 and 150 member firms went out of business and/or merged with other firms. The paperwork crisis by itself did not cause all of the failures, but the firms that failed (or merged) primarily had too little automation and inadequate capitalization for the growing market. Once again, the NYSE and its member organizations provided more than $100 million to pay to the customers of firms that liquidated. Much of this assistance was provided in the same way that Haupt & Co. was bailed out in 1963 (see entry for 11/22/1963). This was another function assumed by the SIPC when it was created by Congress in 1970.

December 31, 1969— On this date, the Dow Jones closed the year and the decade at 800.4, compared to 679.4 on 12/31/59, the last day of the 1950s. Thus the Dow had an increase of nearly 18 percent for the decade of the 1960s. It had exactly quadrupled from the 200.1 at which it ended the 1940s. An increase of four times in 20 years represented great growth in the stock market, and the Dow had even reached a high for the 1960s of 995.15 on 2/9/1966. But it was unable to crack the famous 1,000 mark. The Dow would spend several weeks over 1,000 during the 1970s, but it would also fall as low as 577.6 in 1974, a drop of 45 percent from its decade-high of 1,051.7 in 1973 (see entry for 1/11/1973).

This drop of 45 percent in less than a year was one of the biggest drops in history over such a short time. The Dow, of course, had several bigger drops between the fall of 1929 and the summer of 1932. President Nixon resigned in disgrace in 1974, and the ongoing effects of the oil embargo at that time were the main reasons for the 1974 drop. Essentially, the Dow Jones average would flail up and down in the 1970s before starting another big climb upward in the early 1980s and the full decade of the 1990s.

March 26, 1970— Public ownership of member firms was approved by the NYSE for the first time. This meant that the member firms could issue their own stock to the public. Donaldson, Lufkin & Jenrette became the first member firm to do so on 4/9/1970.

February 8, 1971— The NASDAQ automated quote system was announced by NASD. The NASD is the National Association of Securities Dealers, a group that for many decades was known as the "over-the-counter" market. The NASD simply added an "AQ" for Automated Quotation to the end of their name to create what was to become a famous acronym, NASDAQ. However, the NASD now states that "NASDAQ" simply means Nasdaq, i.e., it is no longer an acronym. As a result, in these pages the term "Nasdaq" without the capitals will refer to both the Nasdaq market and the operation behind it.

In 1921, when the New York Curb Exchange moved indoors (see entry for 1/5/1953), the brokers handling the smallest companies began to organize to trade mainly the stocks of companies not listed on the then two big exchanges, the NYSE and the Curb. Then in 1934, the newly created SEC (see entry for 6/6/1934) put pressure on the various firms on Wall Street to organize into more formal organizations. In response, the firms formed a trade group that was eventually called the National Association of Securities Dealers (NASD). This organization was officially recognized when Congress passed the Maloney Act in 1938. It is ironic that pressure from the SEC produced the NASD, and, as we shall see in a minute, also produced the Nasdaq. This is because the SEC represents the government, and the government is always pushing for additional competition in all marketplaces. In the case of the Nasdaq, the government got far more competition than they bargained for, which in their view is a very good thing. In spite of being formally organized under the acronym NASD, the dealers in the organization were still known to the general public as the over-the-counter market until the creation of the Nasdaq in 1971. It wasn't long before everyone recognized that this thing called the Nasdaq was a very powerful new marketplace.

By the 1990s, the Nasdaq grew bigger than the NYSE in terms of trading volume, and in 1997, it announced the opening of an on-line service that could provide information to the executives of companies listed on the Nasdaq about the trading of not only their stocks, but the trading of the stocks of their competitors. At this point, the Nasdaq was definitely the star of the show in the public's mind because the Nasdaq index was soaring. We'll address the growth of the Nasdaq in our tracking of the great bull market of the 1990s.

At its beginning in 1971, a major advantage of the Nasdaq was that its commissions were flexible, based on a very sensible system in which bigger trades had lower percentage commissions. Obviously, the amount of work done to trade 10,000 shares is not much different from that needed to trade 1,000 shares, and in a competitive environment, a 10,000 share trade should have a smaller percentage commission (even if a higher total commission). This fact was not lost on the SEC, and it was a major reason that they had supported the effort to create the Nasdaq. As soon as the Nasdaq began appearing on the screens of brokers across the country, the NYSE realized that the jig was up. The NYSE had resisted changing the fixed commission system that it had used since the 1790s. When the SEC directed the NYSE to establish a system of negotiated commissions on trades involving more than $500,000, the NYSE realized that eventually they would have to go "all the way." The government gave the NSYE four more years to adopt a fully negotiated commission for all trades. The NYSE dragged its feet for the whole four years, but eventually the fixed commission system was scrapped (see entry for 5/1/1975).

The NYSE and the Nasdaq are by far the top exchanges in the world, and have been competing heavily since this date in 1971. The NYSE achieved its high position after more than 200 years of operation. The Nasdaq essentially sprang nearly full-blown from this date in 1971, although the over-the-counter companies (NASD) that came together to produce the Nasdaq have been trading for over a century themselves. The Nasdaq, however, still has a "hangover" in the sense that its over-the-counter predecessors operated under a small cloud of shady dealings.

It took the Nasdaq less than 20 years to become the third biggest market in the world (behind the NYSE and the Tokyo stock market) in terms of the number of companies having their shares traded in the marketplace, and less than five more years to rise to the top exchange in terms of the volume of shares traded. However, the questions about some of its operating methods remain. There were instances in the "crash" of 1987 where many Nasdaq dealers left their offices at the peak of the panic or refused to answer the phone, leaving investors who wanted to sell their Nasdaq stocks out in the cold (see entry for 10/19/1987 for the results of this practice).

Many of the problems with the Nasdaq were initially overlooked because the Nasdaq has produced great returns for its investors. It grew from a level of 100 at its inception on this date to just over 5,000 in the year 2000, an increase of 50 times. Those happy traders who rode the Nasdaq up didn't wish to hear any bad stories about its questionable upbringing. However, when the Nasdaq "bubble" (I use the word deliberately) burst in 2000, and the Nasdaq fell by a huge 60 percent in just one year between 2000 and 2001, the traders who rode the Nasdaq roller coaster down would have plenty of their own bad stories to tell.

In spite of the bursting of the Nasdaq bubble, in the summer of 2001 it still stood near 2,000, an increase of 20 times since it was born in 1971. For comparison, the Dow stood at 882 on the day the Nasdaq was born, and thus the Dow increased about 13 times by the year 2000, while the Nasdaq was increasing 50 times. Moreover, following the crash of the Nasdaq, the Dow remains near an increase of less than 12 times since 1971, while the Nasdaq holds on to its increase of 20 times. But this long view has been ignored by investors who felt the 60 percent drop between 2000 and 2001, which wiped many of them out, was caused by unethical and even illegal practices by many analysts who were active in the Nasdaq arena of small companies, especially the Internet companies. This issue is addressed in the final pages of this book.

Beyond this issue, there has been an interesting duel between the NYSE and the Nasdaq during the past 30 years.

February 18, 1971— On this date, the NYSE itself was incorporated as a not-for-profit corporation. Of course, its members were still very much for-profit organizations.

July 27, 1971— Merrill Lynch, then the biggest brokerage firm, became the first member firm to have its own stock listed on the NYSE. Incidentally, considering the dramatic increases in volume that have taken place over the years, Merrill Lynch, along with the other top brokerage firms, has turned out to be a great investment.

August 15, 1971— President Nixon, at the end of a television speech announcing wage and price controls for 90 days, dropped a bombshell by removing the dollar from the gold standard, thus devaluating the dollar. Economists have argued for decades about the effects of this change, which the magazine *Fortune* in 1991 called a "misbegotten decision that is still costing us, and the world, dearly." However, the markets in the United States were not as enamored with gold as the European markets have been over the centuries, and neither at that time nor today do Americans really care much about the gold standard. This devaluation has been blamed for the sharp rise in oil prices declared by the Organization of Petroleum Exporting Countries (OPEC) in early 1973, and the subsequent inflation that followed. But the day after the announcement, the trading volume on the Exchange was a then-record 31 million shares, and the Dow gained 32 points to close at 889. As ever, investors were worried about today, not the vague future, even if the "future" would come much sooner than they anticipated.

July 13, 1972—A board of directors, including 10 members from the "public" (as opposed to members of the NYSE) among its 21 members, replaced the NYSE's more stuffy-sounding board of governors, which had a total of 33 members. This was an honest attempt by the NYSE to make an organizational change that would strengthen the role of public investors and listed companies in governing the NYSE. Concurrently, James J. Needham became the first full-time, salaried chairman of the NYSE, joining the president of the NYSE in this distinction. It was hoped these changes would make the NYSE more responsive to the public's needs. The new group of 21 directors included 10 leaders from the securities industry, 10 representatives of the public, and a salaried chairman. Continuing its drive to appear more responsive to the public, the new board held some of its monthly meetings outside of New York.

November 14, 1972—On this date, the Dow passed the magic 1,000 mark for the first time. One month later, it hit its high for the year of 1972 at 1,036.

January 11, 1973—Continuing its rise, the Dow hit a new all-time high at 1,051.7. This turned out to be the high for 1973 and for the decade of the 1970s. By December of 1973, the Dow would be more than 263 points lower (down exactly 25 percent). The market varied by nearly 2-to-1 during the decade, as noted in the entry for 12/31/1969.

May 11, 1973—The Depository Trust Company was established by the NYSE on this date. It was intended to provide a central depository for securities certificates and to permit the transfers of stock ownership to be made electronically. The DTC replaced the Central Certificate Service (CCS) that had been created by the NYSE in 1968. The CCS was considered a great leap forward in eliminating the physical handling of certificates in permitting transfers to be made electronically. The DTC went several steps further in this process. This is one example of the type of change that the NYSE was making on all fronts to eliminate the physical handling of documents. In this way, the ever growing volume of trading could be handled electronically.

October 1, 1974— Today the NYSE extended its closing time to 4:00 P.M., setting the trading hours of the Exchange at 10:00 A.M. to 4:00 P.M. It would not be the last change in hours, because the demands of the investors would require more trading time to handle the resulting volume.

May 1, 1975— This was the first official day on which fixed commissions were eliminated. This date had been viewed with dread by the NYSE for the last four years (see entry for 2/8/1971). Accordingly, it was known as "Mayday," and many brokers predicted the end of civilization as they knew it. From the time of the Buttonwood Tree Agreement in 1792 (see entry for 5/17/1792) until this date, 183 years later, Exchange members had been required to charge their customers specified minimum commission rates on buy and sell orders. It was not lost on the brokers that Tokyo and a number of other markets in Asia and Europe were still continuing the practice of fixed commissions. The brokers couldn't believe the NYSE was going ahead with such a (in their opinion) devastating change. However, the change was necessary.

But aside from the competition from the Nasdaq and pressure from the SEC, the increase in the size of orders on the NYSE had grown far beyond anything the NYSE had ever expected. Institutional investors, both on their own behalf and on the behalf of such organizations as pension funds, had begun to place large orders much more frequently. Orders as large as 10,000 or more shares had a frequency of nine such transactions daily on the NYSE in 1965. By 1975, the number had increased to 136 a day; by the early 1990s, there would be 3,500 a day, and the number would increase further during that decade. Objectively, one had to agree that the nature of the market had changed.

Further, the flexible commissions on the Nasdaq were attracting institutional business as well as non-members of the NYSE (the so-called "third" and "fourth" markets) who were making trades outside of the NYSE on the once-disdained "over-the-counter" market. NYSE management saw the handwriting on the wall, even if many of their member firms did not. The phasing out of fixed commissions began with the advent of the Nasdaq in 1971 and continued in steps until the infamous "Mayday" arrived when all fixed commissions ceased (except for very small orders that totaled below $2,000).

One major member firm had argued that Mayday might result in the failure of as many as 200 regional brokerage firms. Contrary to what might be thought about this "fearmongering," his forecast turned out to be on the low side. With the arrival of Mayday, commission rates on institutional orders fell 40 percent. Wall Street responded just like any other type of business faced with a new set of rules. The brokers began immediately to sort themselves into "discount brokers" offering bare bones service and low rates, while other brokers became "full service" firms, offering a wide range of service and charging commissions not far from the previous rates. Unsurprisingly the brokers found that the more competitive environment, in which the customers knew they could negotiate commission rates, provoked an immediate surge in trading (if you cut the price, they will come). There were other factors involved, of course, but average daily trading volume on just the NYSE has surged more than 800 percent in the years since Mayday and the elimination of fixed rates.

Looking back from today, with nearly all stock markets completely computerized, no one could imagine a time when people would try to trade stocks with fixed commissions. Certainly, "day trading" would be impossible in such an environment. It may be hard to imagine what the fuss was all about, but if you do anything without change for more than 180 years, any change is, almost by definition, wrenching.

June 16, 1975 — On this date, the full consolidated tape was introduced. The full consolidated tape combined trades for all NYSE listed stocks from all markets on one tape. This was a fundamental step forward in developing a national market system.

March 1, 1976 — The Designated Order Turnaround (DOT) system was inaugurated on this date. This was a fully automated system which was intended primarily to route smaller orders from member firms to the Exchange floor. Then, the return execution reports would be sent back to the firms electronically. In terms that most people today could understand, the major advantage of the system was that an investor phoning his order to his broker could stay on the line and quickly receive a verbal confirmation, not an "I'll call you back as soon as possible," which of course would turn out to be the next day at soonest.

Today, the vast majority of NYSE orders are routed electronically to the floor through SuperDot, the system that, in 1984, superseded the initial DOT system. It was this kind of ongoing change that enabled the NYSE to handle what only recently were considered incredible volumes. For example, in

1968, a number of brokerage firms went out of business because of their inability to handle daily volumes of 17 million shares. In a year, the industry was handling up to 24 million shares daily, and with the advent of the DOT system, 30 million shares were being easily handled on a daily basis.

Following additional technological advances in using computers, the activity levels expanded almost literally without end. During the crash of 1987 (see entries for 10/1987), as the market dumped a record loss of 508 points on the brokers on the day of October 19, 1987, it also dumped a trading volume of over 600 million shares. In an attempt to make a comeback on the following day, it dumped another 600 million shares on the brokers. There were the expected problems in handling a sudden 20:1 increase in volume during the crash of 1987, but generally the DOT system held up. The industry then held a successful demonstration in 1990 to show it could handle 800 million shares a day. However, by the end of the 1990s, the volumes were routinely running at 1 billion shares a day. The peak went over 2 billion in 2001, but by then even that level hardly caused a flutter on the NYSE (the Nasdaq was regularly doing higher volumes than the NYSE by then). It was improvements like the DOT system that got the NYSE into the billion volume range with apparent ease. It is really necessary to congratulate the NYSE on its ongoing efforts in computerizing not only its own systems, but those of the thousands of member firms that work with the NYSE. The manner of trading at the end of the century was certainly different than at the beginning, and the major focus today is on such things as day trading and the proliferation of dot-com companies. But one of the biggest changes is the ability of the NYSE to handle billion-share trading days routinely with greatly enhanced accuracy and precision.

It should also be pointed out that around the same time the DOT system was inaugurated in 1976, an Automated Bond System (ABS) was introduced that still handles the vast majority of NYSE bond trades.

March 4, 1976—Alternative listing standards were introduced on this date to facilitate the listing of foreign firms on the NYSE. This was another tiny step by the NYSE in trying to create a truly worldwide market all in one place (at Wall and Broad streets in lower Manhattan).

May 24, 1976—This date marked a little noticed but significant change in the way the NYSE did business. Starting today, the specialists on the trading floor now began to handle "odd lots," purchases of stocks in quantities of fewer than 100 shares. For decades, these kinds of purchases were truly a pain in the neck to brokers. But, for those same decades, buying in odd lots was the primary way individuals bought stocks on the great big NYSE. Because they were a bother to brokers, buyers of stocks in odd lots usually paid a premium price and took delivery whenever they could get it. But the NYSE, ever conscious to continue to reach out to the public, finally got specialists to handle odd lots, thus giving individual investors improved pricing and delivery. It was a victory for the "little guy."

The ability of the specialists to take on this job was an outgrowth of the first electronic specialist "book." A pilot program had been introduced in 1970 to take the specialists' log of all orders awaiting execution out of the format of loose-leaf notebooks and into an electronic display. With such a computerized system, the specialists could electronically enter orders, match buy and sell orders, and generate execution reports automatically. These electronic books have been continually improved and are now used for nearly all stocks.

February 3, 1977— For the first time, foreign brokers and dealers were permitted to obtain membership in the NYSE. As foreign brokers applied for membership, the NYSE took yet another step in becoming a truly international marketplace.

April 17, 1978— The Intermarket Trading System (ITS) started functioning on this date. The ITS provides an electronic link between the NYSE and its competing exchanges in the United States. In this way, brokers can access all markets nationwide to find the best buy or sell price for a security. In a sense, this was an amazing development for the NYSE because an order that might have previously been executed on the NYSE could be executed on a competing exchange if the price at that moment was better. One might wonder why the NYSE would take such a step. The answer, as it usually is in such situations, is that the government published the Securities Act Amendments in 1975. In its never ending quest for more competition, it mandated what it called a national market system. The response to this mandate was the ITS.

The ITS began operation in nine markets; i.e., nine different exchanges. These included the American, Boston, Cincinnati, Midwest (Chicago), New York, Pacific and Philadelphia Stock Exchanges, the Chicago Board Options Exchange, and, of course, the Nasdaq. Eleven stocks made up the initial list of issues available for ITS trading. However, by the early 1990s, 2,306 issues were involved in the ITS, and the number continues to grow.

The ITS included a consolidated electronic tape that combined the last sale price from all markets. There was no longer a tape exclusively for transactions on the NYSE. However, even under these circumstances, through the end of the 1980s, when the NYSE and the Nasdaq began their battle for domination in earnest, the NYSE dominated the number of issues in ITS in the sense that over 80 percent of the stocks in the ITS system were listed on the NYSE. The simple reason for this was the fact that NYSE issues tended to be the most widely held and most active stocks, and it is not surprising that the other markets would find these stocks the most desirable to trade. The NYSE stood as the largest and most technologically advanced securities exchange, offering the highest degree of liquidity. That means that nearly 85 percent of all NYSE stocks that traded in all markets ended up being traded on the NYSE. This was the foundation from which the NYSE intended to meet the challenge of the Nasdaq in the 1990s.

October 6, 1979— Paul Volker, the new chairman of the Federal Reserve, made his first increase in the interest rate on this date. This was Volker's first step in trying to reign in inflation, and in a new activist Fed policy that would run through the rest of the century. Volker would increase interest rates to record levels to arrest the record inflation rate, and although Volker would prove to be successful in doing so, the legacy of the high inflation Volker would trying to subdue would cost Jimmy Carter his presidency in 1980. When Volker stepped down in 1987, Alan Greenspan would become the new chairman. Greenspan would say all the correct things about keeping inflation in check, but the first thing he would do was flood the market with money after the 1987 crash. This would be the correct thing to do at the time, but it would slowly begin to appear over the years that Greenspan would use interest rate reductions to help the stock market, rather than just trying to manage the economy. "Uncle" Alan would be perceived as a Fed chairman who would not let outside events hurt the stock market. In this way he would help the infamous Nasdaq bubble to grow during the 1990s whether he intended to do so or not. Perception is reality in the eyes of the perceiver.

December 31, 1979— The Dow ended the decade of the 1970s at 838.74. Since it had ended the 1960s at an even 800, this was an overall gain of less than five percent for the Dow during the decade of the 1970s. As mentioned before (see entry for 12/31/1969), the Dow varied from high to low by a factor of nearly two to one during the 1970s, but it barely budged between the beginning and end of the decade.

As it entered the 1980s, the NYSE attempted to expand its activities by entering the futures market. It created a separate subsidiary, named the New York Futures Exchange (NYFE), and began selling futures on its own NYSE Composite Index and other types of financial futures. But the NYSE was a distant third in this type of trading behind the Chicago Board of Options and even the American Stock Exchange, which had actively pursued the options market. Since this book is about the *stock* exchange, we will not pursue dealings in the great number of futures and other financial products that were created in the next two decades. As an aside, the NYSE never made a success of the options business and finally sold it to the very successful Chicago options operation in the late 1990s.

The point to be made here is that the great success of the NYSE in producing an effective and efficient market for stocks did not automatically mean that it could successfully take the lead in dealing with other financial products. Once more, it is a case of "each shoemaker to his own last."

April 21, 1980— This was a significant date for our old friend the *Wall Street Journal.* It was announced on this date that by the end of 1979 the *Wall Street Journal* had become the nation's largest newspaper in terms of circulation. It continued to grow into early 1980, and it had reached a circulation of 1.9 million, giving it an even larger lead in the circulation wars. It ostensibly could have had an even larger circulation by this date, but it was hampered by the lack of newsprint in the United States. The result was that it had to turn down advertising, an event that creates bitter tears at any newspaper. The acorn planted by Eddie Jones and Charles Dow had indeed turned into a giant oak. It was certainly another sign that the public could not get enough of the stock market.

November 13, 1980— The Nasdaq closed over 200 for the first time on this date. This meant that the Nasdaq had doubled in the nearly ten years since it was created in early 1971 (see entry for 2/8/1971). The Dow was at 982 on this date, up only 11 percent from the 882 level at which the Dow stood when the Nasdaq was born. This was only a small milestone in the battle between the Nasdaq and the Dow, which would continue through the next two decades.

August 18, 1982— On this day, 132,681,120 shares were traded on the NYSE. This was the first 100 million share day in NYSE history. The ability of the NYSE to trade 100 million shares was partly due to upgrades of the trading floor that took place from 1979 through 1981. In order to install new trading posts incorporating the latest electronic technology without interrupting trading, the 14 new posts were built on a platform suspended over the trading floor. When the new posts were ready, workers started every Friday night to dismantle an old post and lower a new post into place, so it would be ready for trading on Monday morning. This went on for 14 successive Fridays, after which the 14 new posts were operating on the floor. No trading time was lost during the transition. The service lines for the new posts (power distribution, air conditioning, and signal cables) remained suspended 30 feet in the air above the trading post.

In 1984, the NYSE went on to have its first 200 million share day. But this will be one of the last milestones noted herein because volume soared to over 600 million during the 1987 crash (see entry for 10/19/1987) and grew regularly through the 1990s and into 2000. The NYSE now routinely trades over 1 billion shares per day, getting up to a record 2 billion at its peak. Also, as mentioned before, the Nasdaq regularly reports volumes greater than those of the NYSE, although if the NYSE calculated volume in the way the Nasdaq does, NYSE volumes might appear higher (see entry for 2/8/1996). At any rate, stock market volumes ballooned so quickly in the 1990s, and are now routinely so high, that lower level milestones do not really provide useful information.

November 6, 1984— The NYSE stayed open on Election Day for the first time on this date, and from a business standpoint, the change of practice was rewarded with the reelection of Ronald Reagan, who was a good friend of business.

March 28, 1985— Ronald Reagan was the first President to visit the NYSE while still in office.

May 6, 1985— The Nasdaq closed over the 300 mark today. The Nasdaq had been above 300 during the trading day in prior years, but it never quite closed over 300, and the level at closing is how milestones of this type are marked. The Nasdaq had now tripled since its creation in 1971. On this day the Dow stood at 1,248, about 40 percent above the level of 882 at which the Dow stood on the day the Nasdaq was created. Thus the Nasdaq had increased three times while the Dow had reached only 1.4 times its size on the 1971 birthday of the Nasdaq.

September 30, 1985— Starting today, the NYSE once more expanded its trading hours, opening a half hour earlier than before. This set the trading hours at 9:30 A.M. to 4:00 P.M., the earliest official trading time for the NYSE since it was created. It was another step in the process to accommodate the public's obsession with trading stocks.

December 11, 1985— Today, the Dow closed over 1,500 for the first time. It had now grown by more than 75 percent in the first six years of the 1980s. As we have noted before, the Dow first reached the magic 1,000 mark on 11/14/1972, but it wandered up and down throughout the 1970s and closed the decade at only 838.74 (see entry for 12/31/1979). However, the Dow topped the 1,100 mark for the first time on 2/24/1983 and began a rapid move upward from that point. It took over 10 years to get from the 1,000 milestone (11/14/1972) to the 1,100 milestone (2/24/1983), but less than three years to get from 1,100 to 1,500. For the record, the Dow first closed over 1,200 on 4/26/1983; over 1,300 on 5/20/1985; and over 1,400 on 11/6/1985.

May 30, 1986— Continuing to try to stay ahead of the Dow in growth rate (actually an easier task at the low absolute levels of the Nasdaq as compared to those of the Dow), the Nasdaq closed over 400 for the first time on this date. However, the Dow had already reached 1,877 by now as it continued to race upwards in the 1980s. This means that, while the Nasdaq had quadrupled from 1971 through this date, the Dow had increased by slightly more than two times in the same period. The Dow was now growing slightly faster than the Nasdaq since we made our comparison in the entry for 5/6/1985.

June 5, 1986— The board of directors of the NYSE was expanded to include 24 outside directors, 12 of whom are public members and 12 of whom are industry members (see 7/13/1972). This was yet another move by the NYSE to attempt to be more responsive to public input.

November 4, 1986— On this date, Ivan Boesky pled guilty to an unspecified criminal count of insider trading. Dennis Levine, an investment banker for Drexel Burnham (which would end up in bankruptcy itself in 1990 due to the Michael Milken affair — see entry for 12/21/1988), confessed that he had passed tips on planned takeovers to Boesky, who could trade the stocks for his own gain. During the relationship between Drexel and Boesky, Drexel eventually raised over $600 million in junk bonds to help Boesky open his own company on the condition that Drexel collect about $24 million in fees.

The details were even more entangled than this, but the bottom line is that Boesky received a 3½ year prison sentence after admitting guilt. However, in a plea bargain, Boesky ended up serving about half of the sentence and paying a $100 million fine. The fact that Boesky turned state's evidence on several other dealers enabled him to get a lighter sentence. One of the famous Wall Street figures fingered by Boesky was Michael Milken, who was the key all-star money maker for Drexel Burnham. The eventual fines for Milken and Drexel Burnham would far outweigh those levied on Boesky (as noted above, see entry for 12/21/1988 for the sorry story of Drexel and Milken).

It should be noted here that there was much more criminal activity going on in the 1980s than that involving Boesky and Milken. These happened to be the men who were caught, and of whom examples were made. But the problems in the 1980s that led to the crash of 1987 were actually no different from the problems of the 1920s that led to the crash of 1929. If one had to pick a single cause for either crash, it was once again pure unadulterated greed. This problem would reappear again in the crash of the Nasdaq in 2000. There is no reason to believe it will ever go away.

But we also have to note that the opportunity to make money in the market, either legally or illegally (or at the least unethically), was a great attraction to many people. In 1987 a seat on the NYSE would sell for a then-record $1.15 million. There was no lack of new entries into the great stock market game, in spite of the aroma coming out of the Boesky affair. As new opportunities appeared in the great bull market of the 1990s, a seat would sell for $2.65 million in 1999, in spite of rumbles about questionable activities going on in the market. Traders were willing to pay whatever it took to get in on the action.

In 1987, Oliver Stone's movie *Wall Street* appeared in December. It starred Michael Douglas in a role (that won Douglas an Oscar) based on Ivan Boesky and his friends. In the film, Douglas makes an impassioned speech in favor of greed. Later, when challenged by a young broker who was once Douglas' dedicated student as to why Douglas/Boesky insisted on "wrecking" a company for a quick profit in spite of the fact that the company might be nursed back to profitability, Douglas replies simply, "Because it's wreckable." It's like the old fable in which a scorpion talks another animal into giving him a ride across a river, the scorpion saying that of course he won't sting the other animal because then they would both die. When the scorpion does deliver the fatal sting after all while the two are subsequently crossing the river, the other animal asks why he did such a self-destructive thing. The scorpion replies simply, "Because it's my nature." And so it is.

The film also shows clearly how dishonest brokers don't hesitate to use dishonest reporters to plant stories to support their intentions. First the broker creates a buying buzz in a stock he's buying at lower levels, then he creates a selling buzz when he's ready to dump the stock at the top of the market, and he makes make a double profit by selling short as the stock falls. The broker is willing to attempt any scam that makes him a profit, while the reporter is willing to take any route that gives him an "exclusive." The naive self-made investor who is hunting for his "share" of all that easy money being made is duped by both the broker and the reporter.

Perhaps the single most frightening thing about the movie is the fact that, as presented in the film, Douglas/Boesky is a compelling character. He is smart and tough and making big money in a market that only he and those like him comprehend clearly. He is someone you can't help but like. The other (honest) characters seem like wimps in comparison. On one hand it seems good to suggest that those brave souls who want to go it alone in the market should be required to see the movie first. But on the other hand, perhaps those watching would learn the wrong lesson. Perhaps it was not a coincidence that the movie appeared in the year of the biggest single one-day crash in the century (which we will detail shortly).

January 8, 1987— Right after the New Year opened, the Dow passed the 2,000 milestone for the first time. The stage was being set for the October debacle. The public was buying stocks that were already quite high by historical standards, compared to their earning potential. Institutions were buying in big blocks, and financiers who concentrated on arbitrage (like Boesky) were reaping big profits. The market would run uphill like an unchallengeable locomotive in the first eight months of the year, and then it would roll back downhill as if it had lost both fuel and brakes.

July 17, 1987— In just six months, the Dow soared from 2,000 in January of 1987 to close over 2,500 for the first time in July of 1987. Everyone assumed that in less than another six months, the Dow would rush past the 3,000 milestone, but as it turned out, it would take until April of 1991 for the Dow to reach 3,000. Ironically, the Nasdaq was climbing to its 1987 high of 456 in the summer of 1987 also, and it was assumed the Nasdaq would soon pass the 500 mark. But the Nasdaq would not get to 500 for the first time until April of 1991, the same month in which the Dow would get to 3,000 for the first time.

Thus, in April of 1991, the Nasdaq would show a five-fold increase during the 20-year period since its inception in February of 1971, while the Dow would show an increase of 3.4 times over the same period. Ten years later, in April of 2001 (after the crash of 2000), the Nasdaq would show an increase of 3.3 times for the ten years since April 1991, while the Dow would show an increase of 3.5 times for those same 10 years. The Nasdaq crash thus brought parity back to the two indexes in terms of the rate of increase for the most recent decade.

August 25, 1987— Today the Dow hit what was then an all-time record high of 2,722.42, an increase of 35 percent for 1987 in just 8 months. This is the peak from which the Dow would drop in stages until Monday, October 19, when it would lose 508 points in one day. On that day the Dow would close at 1,738.7, a loss of 36.1 percent in less than two months. The Nasdaq would accompany the Dow down in its big October dive, but would do little until then.

September 3, 1987— In just nine days, the Dow lost 125 points from its 1987 high, moving back under 2,600 today. In the next 18 days, the Dow would arrive at 9/21/1987 having fallen by another 100 points. It had moved back under 2,500, and had fallen a total of about 222 points or 8 percent from the high it set only 27 days ago. The Dow was throwing off warning signs in every direction, but investors were still hoping it would start moving upwards again. The increasing volumes showed that many new investors had jumped into the market due to the big move upwards in the first eight months of the year, and they were now not sure what to do. A falling market was not what they felt they had been promised.

October 9, 1987— After adding almost 150 points between September first and October first, and pushing back above the 2,600 level, giving hope to investors everywhere, the Dow lost over 150 points in 8 days and fell back to 2,482.21, almost exactly where it had closed on 9/21/1987 before it took its quick jump upwards. Because the Dow was unable to build on or even hold onto its 150 point rebound, storm clouds were now building over stock markets everywhere. More experienced investors started dumping stocks in earnest.

October 14, 1987— On this Wednesday, the Dow dropped another 95 points and volume rose to 207 million shares, a very high level at that time. This indicated that many investors were running for the exits. But it has to be recognized that for every share sold, there had to be a corresponding buyer. And they couldn't all be specialists trying to maintain an orderly market.

October 15, 1987— In a follow-up to yesterday's poor performance, on this Thursday, the Dow lost another 58 points and erased another milestone. It fell back under the 2,400 point level, closing the day at 2,355.09, while volume rose to 263 million shares. The Dow had not been this low since June 10, almost exactly four months earlier, when it closed at 2,353.61. Investors watched anxiously to see how the Dow would close out the week on Friday. The smell of panic was now in the air for those who recognized the odor.

October 16, 1987— This Friday brought no relief to market watchers. The Dow erased yet another milestone, falling below the 2,300 level and closing the day and the week at 2,246.74. This was a drop of 108 points for the day, and volume rose to an all-time high of 338 million shares, a very ominous sign. If one listened closely, the sounds of running feet were everywhere.

The additional loss today brought the total drop of the Dow to over 475 points since the Dow hit its 1987 high of 2,722.42 on August 25. This was a loss of over 17 percent in less than two months. The professionals who had not yet run for the exits, for reasons known only to them, spent the weekend preparing their sell orders for the opening of the NYSE (and other markets worldwide) on Monday, October 19. Others were still willing to wait and watch, but they had no idea how fast the train would speed downhill on Monday once it got well underway.

October 19, 1987 — On what inevitably became known as Black Monday (the NYSE seems to have a "Black" day in its history for every day of the week), the market was deluged with sell orders as soon as it opened. The Dow fell quickly by 200 points in about two hours, then bounced back by about 100 points between 11 A.M. and 1 P.M., while everyone caught their breath and hoped the respite would continue. Just at that moment the slide began again, with computer generated selling programs leading the charge. Small investors were swept away in this mostly institutional landslide. Total volume for the day was 604 million shares, nearly double the prior record that had been set just the previous Friday. But the brand new record itself would last only one day. Volume grew to 608 million shares on Tuesday the 20th (it would take another 10 years, until 1997, before trading volume would get over 700 million shares). This crash was one for the record book in every way.

The 10/19/1987 crash was a very big deal. Not only were records set for the losses suffered (around the world), it was a very sobering experience for many investors that affected the way they operated for a few years. Further, it was a testing time for the competing NYSE and the Nasdaq. The NYSE added to its favorable image, while the new kid on the block, the Nasdaq, came away with a monstrous black eye. These issues affected the operation of the two exchanges in future years.

The Dow fell by a total of about 600 points during the day, then rebounded somewhat at the end of the day to close with a loss of exactly 508 points, or 22.61 percent. Both the absolute point loss and the percentage loss were all-time records for the Dow by large margins. The point loss has since been exceeded as the Dow climbed above the 7,500 level in the 1990s, then on to almost 12,000 in the year 2000. But the 508 point loss is still the fourth largest point loss for the Dow in its history, and it is the only one of the top ten point losses to have taken place before 1997.

The percentage loss for the Dow on 10/19/1987 is still by far the greatest percentage loss for the Dow in history. The 22.61 percent loss on 10/19/87 is almost double the 12.82 percent loss that is in second place. This 12.82 percent loss happened on Monday, October 28th, 1929, the day before the Black Tuesday loss that is still known as the Crash of 1929. But Black Tuesday, October 29, 1929, had a smaller loss than Monday 28, 1929 (see entry for 10/28/1929). Black Tuesday still holds the record for the third biggest percentage loss in Dow history. Its percentage loss came in at 11.73 percent, just behind the 10/28/29 loss. The loss is thus also nearly only half of the 10/19/87 record loss.

For people who track seemingly weird coincidences, the big crash of 1987 came on a Monday that was just 9 days short of exactly 58 years after the Monday, 10/28/1929 crash. Further, if the loss of the 1987 crash is measured from the all-time high that was reached in late August, 1987, the Dow fell by 983.7 points from 2,722.4 on August 25, 1987, to 1,738.7 on October 19, 1987. This is a loss of 36.1 percent in 55 days. In 1929, the Dow fell from what was then its all-time high of 381.2 on September 9, 1929, to 230.1 on October 29, 1929. This is a loss of 39.6 percent in 56 days. Thus, the crashes of 1929 and 1987 were nearly identical in terms of the percentage loss from the new all-time high reached before the crash to the low on "crash" day, just 55/56 calendar days later. It is as if the crash of 1929 simply leaped ahead by 58 years and replicated itself. What happened right after the crash was also quite similar, but what happened in the following few years was as different as it could possibly be.

In 1929, the Dow recovered smartly in the next six months to nearly completely reach its pre-crash level, then swooned in the next two years to bottom out at only 11 percent of its all-time high, i. e., a loss of 89 percent. The depression of the 1930s ground on and on as the Dow fell to its nadir. It took 25 years to regain its all-time high of September, 1929.

However, in 1987, the Dow never again was as low as it was on crash day, 10/19/1987, and it surpassed its all-time high of 8/25/87 in just a little more more than two years. From that point it never looked back as it began its historical climb upwards in the 1990s, producing the biggest and longest bull market in history.

But however large the percentage loss of the Dow on October 19, 1987, was in relative terms to its 1929 crash, other indexes here and abroad took it on the chin to as great an extent as the Dow, or even to a much greater degree than the Dow. We'll discuss the large and unusual Nasdaq loss in a moment. The S&P 500 lost 58 points, or 30 percent of its value, a loss greater than that of the Dow. Combined, the major U.S. indexes loss about 21 percent of their value on average on that Black Day. The Australian stock market lost an astounding 58 percent of its value, and markets in Hong Kong, Singapore, and Mexico followed in line behind Australia with substantial losses of that nature. In all, in just the United States, $500 billion worth of NYSE stock value was wiped out in one day. But for the NYSE, the recovery began immediately.

The Nasdaq recorded its all-time record one day loss of 11.35 percent on October 19, 1987. But rather than recovering to some extent on the next day, October 20, 1987, as the other indexes did, the Nasdaq lost another 9.0 percent. This still ranks as the third biggest percentage loss in Nasdaq history, bringing the two–day loss to 20.35 percent. It is believed that the ongoing loss in the Nasdaq was due to the dismal performance of some of its traders on October 19, 1987.

Martin Mayer, who has written over 20 nonfiction books, with about half of those on business and finance, wrote a book called *Markets* devoted almost exclusively to the 1987 crash and its effects around the world. In a section comparing the performance of the specialists on the NYSE to the "market makers" on the Nasdaq in terms of maintaining orderly markets, Mayer had this to say: "The fact is that when the markets collapsed in October 1987, almost the only place that a man with shares of stock could sell them for cash was on the floor of the NYSE, because in the end the specialists took their responsibilities seriously." In comparison, "where the unlisted securities are traded over the telephone and through the [computer] screens, many over-the-counter dealers took the telephone off the hook." According to Mayer, one NYSE specialist signed a check for $26 million to cover the losses his firm had suffered trying to maintain markets on October 19th. The NYSE made its markets with a strong sense of responsibility. The market makers on the Nasdaq ran and hid.

The Nasdaq did bounce back on October 21 when it recorded a gain of 7.34 percent, still its fourth best percentage gain ever. But it wiped this gain off the books with another 9.0 percent loss on October 26, still its fourth worse ever. Thus the Nasdaq suffered three of its four highest percentage losses in conjunction with the October 1987 crash (the other member of the top four did not arrive until April of 2000, when the Nasdaq bubble had burst and the Nasdaq was melting away). The Nasdaq lost nearly 40 percent from its October high to its October low in 1987.

The Nasdaq lost as much or more in terms of prestige in the crash of 1987. In an attempt to prevent its market makers from ignoring customers, especially small customers, the Nasdaq made use of its Small Order Execution System (SOES) mandatory for orders up to 1,000 shares. This system permitted automated execution of small orders without the intervention of market makers. But SOES eventually became a victim of so-called SOES bandits. The bandits would split orders to get under the 1,000 limit and use the fast answers on SOES to make arbitrage profits on price quotes from regular market makers. It was just another example of the pool hall odors remaining in the Nasdaq as it rose to the top.

This a hard problem for the Nasdaq to solve. Until the October 1987 debacle, the Nasdaq was advertised as "The Stock Market of Tomorrow — Today," and exchanges in London and Asia had selected it as the model for their planned electronic exchanges. In the 1990s the Nasdaq used "The Stock Market for the Next 100 Years" as its motto, taking a jab at the NYSE which was celebrating its 200 year anniversary. But several reporters turned the Nasdaq motto into the phrase "The Stock Market for the Next 100 Years — with time off for good behavior."

October 20, 1987— In what would become a common event in the years ahead, early on October 20, 1987, the day after the crash, Fed Chairman

Alan Greenspan announced emergency reserves were available to any bank that needed them. The Fed began to flood the proper channels with money. The recovery from the crash of 1987 was about to begin by the time most brokers who took part in it were just getting up for their early morning cup of coffee. The biggest gainers as a result of the Fed announcement were banks that initially panicked when margin calls put a strain on their support for their broker accounts. But the maximum margin rate (also set by the Fed) was only 50 percent in 1987, as compared to 90 percent in 1929. Thus, with the help offered by the Fed, the margin issue was not nearly as serious as it had been in 1929.

Even though banks were slow to respond to the prodding by the Fed, the 1987 crash continued to follow the pattern of the 1929 crash. The Dow bounced right back the day after the crash. In 1987, the Dow gained 102.27 points on Tuesday, the 20th of October, and the "happier" volume of 608 million broke the record just set on Monday the 19th.

October 21, 1987 — Having convinced themselves that the world was not going to end after all, investors on Wednesday the 21st pushed the Dow up another 186.64 points. This was a percentage gain of 10.15 percent, still the fourth biggest percentage gain in history for a single day, and the last daily percentage gain for the Dow that registered in double digits. The Dow thus had gained almost 289 points in the two days following the crash, a gain of 16.6 percent for the two days. The Dow closed the day at 2,027.85, back over the 2,000 mark again.

October 26, 1987 — The Monday following after the big Monday crash. After closing the previous Friday the 23rd at 1,950.76, the Dow lost 156.83 points on Monday the 26th to close at 1,793.93. This was a percentage loss of 8.04 percent, which still ranks as the eighth biggest one day percentage loss in the history of the Dow. Obviously investors had had two bad weekends back-to-back worrying about what was going to happen when the market opened on Monday. But the Dow had at least remained above its 10/19/1987 low close, and the Dow generally rose for the rest of the year from its low point of today.

December 3, 1987 — The Dow closed today at 1,766.4. This was first close under 1,800 since 10/26/1987, but it still remained above its low of 10/26/1987 (and thus above its low point following the 10/19/1987 crash). December 1987 is still the last month the Dow had a closing level in the 1,700s, so this day represents the lowest close for the Dow through the summer of 2001. The Dow was headed upwards from here, only about 6 weeks after the crash.

December 23, 1987 — The Dow closed at 2,005.6, the highest close for the month of December, 1987. Ironically, the highest close for the month of December, 1986, was 1,955.6. If one looked only at the closing highs at the end of each year, one could assume absolutely nothing happened to the Dow in 1987. It would have seemed to be a dull year.

December 31, 1987 — The Dow closed its tumultuous year at 1,938.3. The low for 1988 would come on January 20, 1988, only 3 weeks later, when the Dow closed at 1,879.14. The Dow would close 1988 at 2,168.6, and it would close 1989 ahead of the then all-time high it had set in August of 1987. The crash of 1987 was completely over in just a little more than two years. After fully recovering in such a short time, the Dow would set out on its decade long run of the longest bull market ever. In this sense, as noted above, there was no comparison at all between the crash of 1929 and that of 1987. In 1929 the pre-crash high wasn't reached again for 25 years, and there was a great desert in between. In 1987, the pre-crash high was regained in only two years, and flowers bloomed in every investor's garden for more than a decade after the crash had been swallowed up and forgotten.

The key questions to be answered about the crash of 1987 are what caused the crash, and what was learned from it. The question of cause was hotly debated at the time, and it was the subject of a report by the "Brady Commission" put together by President Reagan. Numerous articles at the time analyzed the crash, and as noted above, financial writer Martin Mayer wrote one complete book about the crash of 1987, describing what happened at various markets around the world as the crash descended. Suffice it to say that nearly everyone had different — and often contrary — conclusions about the cause. The one I prefer is that another stock market bubble was created by market professionals in a number of ways (legal and illegal or at least unethical) to help them improve their already high profits, and the public came rushing in, following the scent of something for nothing. The public has a stronger scent for something for nothing than any shark has for the smell of blood in the water. When the amateurs came running to something they didn't understand well, that was the impetus for the professionals to grab the fleecing shears and ultimately pop the bubble. The same thing happened in 1929, and the same thing would happen in the Nasdaq crash of 2000. The crash of 1987 was no exception to the rule. In a word, the cause of all such crashes is greed. That is one thing that is never in short supply in the world.

One additional thing we learned, as Mayer pointed out, is that the "old" NYSE, built step by step over two centuries, met its obligations to the best of its considerable abilities. The newcomers in the Nasdaq (and also in the options market) ran and hid. There are substantial signs that the same thing happened in a different way in 2000.

December 21, 1988 — The other shoe dropped with a considerable thud on this date when Drexel Burnham Lambert agreed to plead guilty to six violations of federal law, including insider trading. They agreed to pay penalties of $650 million, the largest such sum ever to that date. Drexel's biggest star was Michael Milken, who had almost literally single handedly created the junk bond industry.

A junk bond is one which has a poor rating (or no ratings at all) by such prestigious rating agencies as Standard and Poor's and Moody's, Inc. This means by conventional standards such a bond is more likely to default, and thus it must pay a high interest rate to attract investors. After careful study, Milken found that such bonds default at a much lower rate than such high interest rates would predict, and a large enough group of such bonds would easily pay enough interest to cover the costs of an occasional default. He sold the industry on his research and thus made it possible for many small companies to get started with "junk" bonds when they had no other source of start-up capital.

Junk bonds also seemed to many savings and loan (S&L) companies an easy way to increase their profits and thus the yield they could pay to depositors, which would make them much more competitive in the market place. It seemed like a good idea at the time, but it ended in disaster for many. On August 9, 1989, President Bush would have to sign a measure to rescue the S&L industry, and many small investors would lose much of their savings.

Of course, junk bond marketing efforts were expensive, and Milken/Drexel collected high commissions for their efforts. Preferring the glitz of Hollywood to the hustle and bustle of Wall Street, Milken and his group worked on the West Coast, almost independently of Drexel back east. Milken could afford the high life. His group got 2 percent as their commission on their junk bond sales. That may not sound like much, but if Drexel, for example, underwrote $200 billion worth of junk bonds over a given time period, Milken's group got a cool $4 billion. Even by today's standards that's a lot of money.

Milken had to share the commission with his group, but estimates were that he made $600 million a year for himself. Once again, a lot of money, especially in the late 1980s. One of Milken's big mistakes, other than being tempted into making even more income by illegal means, was rubbing his riches in the public's face, so to speak. He and Drexel organized a series of amazingly well-named "Predator's Balls," which included Hollywood swells, where once a year an assortment of financial officials and free-loading politicians (are there any other kind?) came together to pursue Hollywood's most attractive sweet young things under the pretense of discussing junk bonds. All tax deductible, of course.

But the fun vanished quickly when one cause of the 1987 crash was claimed to be the machinations in the junk bond industry. When the savings and loan crisis was also laid at the feet of the misuse of junk bonds, Drexel was on the way to collapse. When the public became aware of the size of the funds flowing to Drexel and its most conspicuous all-star, Milken, and when the source of those funds was claimed to be illegal activities that punished small investors, Milken quickly became a hated man. The situation was similar to the one early in the century when abuse was heaped on the original J. D. Rockefeller when he was targeted as a symbol of all that was wrong with trusts. Both cases were also similar in that the public easily swallowed the accusations, and didn't want to be bothered with the facts.

It was claimed that Ivan Boesky got an apparently light sentence (see entry for 11/4/1986) because he was willing to talk and the government was after bigger fish. After Drexel was walloped with its big fines, it began to run short of capital and finally filed for bankruptcy in February of 1990.

The biggest fish was caught a month later when Milken himself was indicted in March 1990 on nearly 100 counts of racketeering. This huge lump of indictments came after Milken refused to plead guilty to two counts of fraud. Finally giving up, he pled guilty on the understanding the judge would be lenient in sentencing, as had happened with Boesky. But federal judge Kimba Wood threw not only the book, but also her desk and anything else available at Milken. The sentence was more political than judicial. After taking the trouble to point out that she was not sentencing Milken for the greed of the 1980s, she proceeded to sentence him for the greed of the 1980s. Milken got 10 years.

In addition, Milken was fined a total of more than $1 billion dollars, $200 million of which was due at sentencing. The $100 millon paid by Boesky was definitely chicken feed. In Drexel and Milken, Boesky gave the government a much bigger fish indeed — the great blue whale in fact. Milken was finally released on probation after serving about three years in prison.

Milken is still a controversial figure. Supporters claim he created a valuable new source of cash for start-up companies that went on to create an uncounted number of jobs. The junk bond industry still thrives today for this purpose. In comparison, the IPO (Initial Public Offering) industry that brought so many new companies into existence in the 1990s (many of which subsequently failed taking all of their investors' money with them) is a process so filled with corruption that it makes Milken look like a naive kid playing in a sandbox.

Milken's supporters also point out that the charges against him were burdened with technicalities. If he had fought the case, he probably never would have been convicted. Or at worst he could have accepted a plea bargain with much better terms than those he got from Kimba Wood, who made him the poster boy for the naughty doings on Wall Street in the 1980s (and maybe for all those done during the century). His major crime was being clever enough to create a new industry no one else had taken the time to discover before.

His detractors claim simply he was an arrogant rich kid who ignored the common folk and got just what he deserved. Who knows?

December 29, 1989 — The Dow closed the year and the decade at 2,753.2, compared to 838.7 at the end of 1979. The gain for the 1980s was 3.3 times or +230 percent in spite of the 1987 crash.

April 12, 1991 — The Nasdaq went over 500 for the first time on this date.

April 17, 1991 — Five days later, the Dow went over 3,000 for first time. As noted briefly in the entry for 7/17/1987, when the Nasdaq passed 500 this month, it marked a five-fold increase since its inception 20 years earlier in 1971. For comparison, when the Dow passed 3,000 this month, it marked an increase of 3.4 times in the Dow since the birth of the Nasdaq. The Nasdaq was well ahead of the Dow in growth at this point in 1991.

The Nasdaq would soar to a peak of 5,132 in March 2000, while the Dow would "only" get to 11,723 at its peak in January 2000. At their peaks, compared to April of 1991, the Nasdaq would be up by 10.3 times, and the Dow would be up by 3.9 times. A gigantic edge to the Nasdaq.

However, almost exactly 10 years after our comparison point of 4/12/1991, in early April 2001, the Nasdaq would be down to 1,638. This would be a huge drop of 68 percent from its peak only 13 months earlier. This left the Nasdaq with an increase of 3.3 times in the 10 years since 4/12/1991.

Almost exactly 10 years after our comparison point of 4/17/1991, the Dow was at 10,400 in mid-April, 2001. This left the Dow with an increase of 3.5 times in the 10 years since 4/17/1991. The Dow was now ahead of the Nasdaq in terms of growth in the decade between April of 1991 and April of 2001. Of course, the ratios now change daily as the stocks fluctuate up and down. But for that 10 year snapshot between their respective milestones in April 1991 and their positions 10 years later, the Dow was a better bet than the Nasdaq in spite of the Nasdaq's big lead at the nine year point. Once upon a time a turtle and a hare had a race...

We'll use the Nasdaq and the Dow to track the amazing bull market of the 1990s. It is necessary to recognize that neither index is an entity of its own. The Dow is an index of 30 selected stocks intended to represent the whole market, even though up to this date all of the Dow stocks are listed on the NYSE. The Nasdaq represents all of the stocks that trade in its purely electronic market place. This gives us a chance to compare the results of the "old economy," as represented by the Dow stocks, to the "new economy" represented by the Nasdaq and its population of Internet and technology stocks.

Both markets grew rapidly through the 1990s, but the Nasdaq formed a huge bubble as the 1990s ended, and burst the bubble in March of 2000. The Nasdaq fell by 68 percent from its maximum (March 2000) to its minimum (April 2001) in just 13 months, and it still was down by 63 percent in August 2001, 17 months after it peaked. It went down and stayed down.

There was no bubble for the Dow. It peaked just after the 1990s ended, and from its maximum to its minimum in the next 18 months it fell by less than 20 percent. For most of those 18 months it has stayed consistently near a loss of only 10 percent from its peak, and it has been within four percent of its peak on several occasions. For the first time in history, there was a crash in one market but not the other. The Dow still has had its two big crashes since 1900, those of 1929 and 1987. But none since. The Nasdaq crashed with the Dow in 1987, but crashed alone in the year 2000.

June 13, 1991— The first NYSE off-hours trading session took place on this date. So-called "crossing" sessions extended the trading activity to 5:15 pm. It was part of the first steps to develop 24 hour trading around the globe if possible.

December 4, 1991— In perhaps the final echo from the S&L junk bond fiascos, Charles Keating was convicted of securities fraud. But to show how difficult it is to make charges of this type stick when the prime accusers are customers who could be accused of acting as if they consisted of equal parts of terminal stupidity and greed, Keating's appeals kept him free for many years, and when he did finally go to jail he got back out on appeal. It took a decade to resolve the case, but Keating finally won.

As long as greed exists to such a high degree in the public, many such cases are going to be reduced to conflicting claims by equally tainted parties. Make no mistake, fraud is present in all facets of the financial industry. But without the greed of the customers who avoid asking questions about deals that appear to be too good to be true, fraudulent deals in many cases would be impossible to complete. Inevitably, however, some people will insist on throwing their life savings into a very murky pot in the belief they can get something for nothing.

January 6, 1992— Ceremonies were held in New York to celebrate the beginning of the bicentennial year of the NYSE.

May 17, 1992— The NYSE celebrated the actual 200th anniversary of the signing of the Buttonwood Agreement (see entry for 5/17/1792).

May 19, 1993— As the bull market of the 1990s got well underway, the Dow went over the 3,500 mark for the first time.

February 23, 1995— In what would later seem like very slow progress, the Dow took nearly two more years to make its next 500-point milestone, as it closed over 4,000 for the first time.

May 22, 1995— The NYSE completed a trading post upgrade as part of its ongoing integrated technology plan (ITP). The NYSE continued to spend large sums to enable its trading floors to handle more volume more efficiently.

June 16, 1995— Taking less than four months to make another 500-point milestone, the Dow closed over 4,500 for the first time. The Dow had grown by nearly 30 percent in the last two years, and by nearly 13 percent in the last four months.

July 17, 1995— The Nasdaq passed a very significant milestone by closing over 1,000 for the first time. The Nasdaq had doubled in just a little over four years. But, as with the Dow, this would seem like very slow progress late in the 1990s.

November 21, 1995— Trying to keep pace with the Nasdaq, the Dow closed over 5,000 for the first time. Thus, the Dow had grown by nearly 70 percent in about 4.5 years.

February 8, 1996— The Dow clicked off another milestone as it closed over 5,500 on this day for the first time. This day was also the twenty-fifth anniversary of the founding of the Nasdaq. This is a good opportunity to compare the overall performances of the two great markets, the NYSE and the Nasdaq. At the end of 1996, the Nasdaq stood alone in the world in competing with the NYSE. The data through 1996 were as follows:

In the year 1996, the NYSE had exactly 50 percent of the dollar volume among all stock markets in the United States. This amounted to $4.1 trillion. The Nasdaq had 40.6 percent or $3.3 trillion. In share volume, the Nasdaq had exactly 52 percent of the total or 138.1 billion shares, an average of 543.7 million shares per day. The NYSE had 39.4 percent of the total or 104.6 billion shares, an average of 412.0 shares per day.

There is a caveat in measuring the differences in trading volume. First, much of the volume generated on the other regional exchanges that exist in the United States (about 6 percent of the total) results from shares whose primary market is the NYSE, but whose final trade may take place on a regional market due to a price edge at closing. Second, the methods of calculating volume on the Nasdaq and the NYSE markets are different. On the floor of the NYSE, a trade is a trade is a trade. On the Nasadaq market, if a customer enters an order to buy shares from a dealer who does not have the stock in inventory, the dealer in turn buys the shares from a market-maker and then resells them to the customer. Each seller must report his trade, and thus the volume reported for that single customer transaction is double what would be reported on the NYSE. How many such trades take place is not recorded, and thus what effect it has on the relative volume is not clear.

This difference in reporting notwithstanding, it still appears that the Nasdaq will continue to record the highest volume of trades, while the NYSE, with its generally higher priced stocks as compared to those on the Nasdaq, will record the highest dollar volume.

The Nasdaq edged past the NYSE in reported trading volume for the first time in 1994. The Nasdaq drew farther ahead in 1995 and was about 32 percent ahead in 1996, as noted in the numbers above. The difference in favor of the Nasdaq was about 23 percent in 1997, and the difference continues generally in that range. The Nasdaq was also the first to go over the one billion mark in daily trading. The Nasdaq hit 1.35 billion on October 28, 1997, while the NYSE first made it over one billion with a mark of 1.22 billion on September 1, 1998. Both exchanges have since had peak days over two billion shares. After all these years, the volume edge goes to the Nasdaq. It certainly has come of age as a leading exchange.

At the end of 1996, there were 3,285 stock issues, representing 2,907 companies, listed on the NYSE. The Nasdaq had 6,384 active securities trading, and there were 5,553 NASD member organizations involved with the Nasdaq, including about 540 registered market makers. The number of NASD member organizations will grow because by law every securities firm doing business with the public must join the NASD, but the number of market makers will grow much more slowly because most NASD members have neither the capital or the desire to be market makers.

Since the NYSE limits itself to 1,366 full members (a limit it has observed since 1953), the NYSE had only 1,427 members at the end of 1996. There were another 61 members who had access to the floor or to the electronic aspects of the NYSE by paying a certain fee, but only 1,366 seat owners. Although this certainly gives the NYSE the flavor of a private club (the first woman was not admitted to membership until December 1967, although there were no specific restrictions against such membership), seats are constantly for sale if you have a few million dollars available and can meet the membership requirements.

The data show that on its twenty-fifth anniversary, the Nasdaq was definitely on equal ground with the NYSE (and the Nasdaq's acquisition of the American Stock Exchange in 1998 confirmed that fact, if any further confirmation was needed). They are different, but definitely equal, organizations. Which one will triumph in the future remains to be seen. The electronic version (the Nasdaq version) of stock exchanges seems to be the wave of the future, as new exchanges overseas and elsewhere continue to copy the Nasdaq model. However, the job of trying to replicate the NYSE seems impossible, so it's not clear if organizations starting from scratch realistically have more than the Nasdaq option to consider. But it is hard to imagine the NYSE fading away. Maybe it will become the NYSE versus the world. If so, don't necessarily bet against the superbly competent NYSE.

October 14, 1996—The Dow closed over 6,000 for the first time. This gain of 500 points (nine percent) took only eight months.

November 15, 1996—Vimpel-Communications became the first Russian company to be listed on the NYSE.

November 25, 1996—The Dow closed over 6,500 for the first time. This time it took only six weeks to achieve another 500-point milestone. Things might be getting out of hand, some began to fear.

December 5, 1996—At the annual dinner of the American Enterprise Institute, Fed chairman Alan Greenspan, the featured speaker, mentioned the terrible collapse of the Japanese Stock Exchange since 1989, and then said that investors in the United States might be demonstrating "irrational exuberance" in their rush to keep bidding shares higher and higher. Ironically, as is often the case, he didn't mention his role in this exuberance in promoting the attitude that "Uncle Alan" would come running to the rescue if anything bad should really happen. Stocks fell in response to a rare "warning" from Greenspan, and fell also when Greenspan raised interest rates in March 1997. But then investors assumed Uncle Alan had just lost his head for a moment, and the market moved upwards again.

February 13, 1997—The Dow showed how much investors were frightened by Greenspan's speech by closing over 7,000. The Dow had now doubled in less than 4 years, an annual rate of return over 18 percent.

June 10, 1997—Galloping ever higher, the Dow closed over 7,500, another gain of 500 points in four months. In what should have been an early warning sign, the Dow had stepped up its recent rate of return to 20 percent. That meant that the Dow was increasing its rate of return even as it moved higher, just the opposite of what one would expect from a normal market.

June 24, 1997 — The NYSE began trading stocks in sixteenths, an interim step towards trading stocks in decimals. Planning to change from trading in eights, which had been going on for nearly two centuries, was not well received by the members of the conservative Exchange.

July 11, 1997 — The Nasdaq closed over 1,500 for the first time. Since April of 1991, when the Nasdaq went over 500 for the first time, the Nasdaq had tripled in just over six years. This was a compound annual return of about 19 percent.

July 16, 1997 — Five days later, the Dow closed over 8,000 for the first time. Since April of 1991, when the Dow closed over 3,000 for the first time, the Dow had not quite tripled as the Nasdaq had done, but the Dow was up by a factor of 2.7, only 10 percent behind the Nasdaq. Thus, so far, both averages had been climbing at nearly the same rate since 1991. This would soon change in favor of the Nasdaq.

October 27, 1997 — On yet another infamous Monday, unsettled international conditions (Thailand, Malaysia, and Hong Kong being at the top of the Asian list) and talk of possible foreign defaults produced a then record point loss of 554.26 points in the Dow. Ironically, this mini-crash came exactly 10 years and eight days after the October 19, 1987 crash that had produced the previous highest one-day point loss (and the highest percentage loss). But the percentage loss on this date was a relatively unremarkable 7.18 percent because the Dow was so much higher in 1997 than in 1987. This percentage loss didn't even make the top 10 in Dow history, even though the point loss was then the all-time record (and still ranks in second place).

Thus, only three months and 11 days after crossing the 8,000 mark, on this day the Dow closed at 7,161.15. This huge loss triggered the "circuit breaker" rule for the first time. The circuit breaker rule was previously established to halt trading after a specified point loss to avoid panic selling. But the rule may have been counterproductive. The first circuit breaker closed the market at 2:35 P.M. when the Dow was down about 350 points. The break caused buyers to disappear, while sellers got ready for the next opening. When trading resumed at 3:05 P.M., the sellers unloaded their stock and the Dow fell another 200 points. When the market closed for the day at 3:30 P.M., the total loss was the record-breaking total of 554.26.

The result of the circuit breaker exercise was a plan to change the break points to values based on percentages rather than absolute points. When the rule was originally written, no one anticipated a Dow at such high levels, or losses of such point magnitudes. The markets developed a new percentage rule by the end of 1997, and it was approved by the SEC in 1998.

Volume on this record-breaking day was also a record breaker on the NYSE, but it was "only" about 700 million (breaking the record of just over 600 million set in the 1987 crash). The really noteworthy volumes came the next day when the markets rebounded.

October 28, 1997 — The Dow followed its record-breaking loss by bouncing back with a record-breaking gain. On this Tuesday, the Dow recorded an all-time high gain of 337.17 points, then by far the best one-day gain in its history (it still ranks as the third best gain, in spite of the much higher levels the Dow would reach in the coming years).

Even more comforting to investors was the fact that the gain came on much higher volume than the then record breaking level that accompanied the loss on the previous day. The volume on this day was about 75 percent higher than the "big" volume of the day before. The NYSE broke through the billion share level for the first time with a trading volume of 1.2 billion shares, a huge jump to its new all-time high. To emphasize the level of enthusiasm that accompanied the rebound in the markets, the Nasdaq also broke through the billion share level for the first time, coming in at an even higher 1.35 billion shares. Both records have since been broken, but they were notable at the time. However, perhaps the most notable item was that the record volume levels were handled with no problems. All the investments in new technology to handle high volume levels had paid off. Today, the average volumes traded every day are equal to or higher than the 1997 records.

The Dow was now back to almost 7,500. It would jump back past 8,000 and then climb above 8,500 in just 4 months. Nothing, it seemed, could stop the bull market of the 1990s.

Alan Greenspan and Treasury Secretary Rubin issued the appropriate soothing words, and President Clinton joined with other Pacific Rim leaders to support a bailout of the Asian nations by the International Monetary Fund (IMF). This time it seemed that the markets were calmed simply by knowing that everyone would try to help them keep flying, with Uncle Alan Greenspan in the lead. But next time, in the 1998 mini-crash in August, they would need to see a little more action from the Fed — and they would get it.

February 27, 1998 — Showing that it had completely overcome the effects of the October 1997 mini-crash, the Dow closed above 8,500 for the first time.

April 6, 1998 — Just five weeks after moving above 8,500, the Dow closed above 9,000 for the first time. The Dow had now tripled in almost exactly seven years, an annual compounded growth rate of more than 16 percent since it hit 3,000.

April 15, 1998 — New circuit breaker rules went into effect after approval by the SEC. The new rules were designed to halt trading when the Dow fell by percentage values of 10, 20, and 30 percent in certain sequences of trading. The new rules almost tripled the point movements required to halt trading as compared to the old rules.

July 16, 1998 — The Nasadaq passed another notable milestone, closing over 2,000 for the first time. The Nasdaq had now quadrupled since April 1991, a compounded annual growth rate of about 20 percent since that time.

August 27, 1998 — The continuing turmoil in Asian countries was joined by turmoil in Russia. The Russian central bank said it would stop intervening to support the ruble. It also stopped dollar trading on the Moscow exchange. The result of these steps was a de facto evaluation. Debt repayments were delayed amid rumors that President Yeltsin would resign. This was too much for markets in all financial products areas. On this Thursday, the Dow dropped 357.36 points, then its third biggest point drop in history (it now ranks only eight). The Dow stabilized a little on Friday, dropping "only" another 116 points. Investors once more decided over the weekend that they didn't like the smell in the air, and they prepared to exit the market.

August 31, 1998 — On this Monday (not called Black Monday this time, although by past standards it certainly qualifies), the Dow dropped by 512.51 points, then the second biggest one-day loss in history behind the drop on 10/27/97 (the 1997 and 1998 drops now rank second and third, respectively on the Dow list). The Dow closed at 7,539.07, just a little less than five months after it passed 9,000 for the first time. This level of the Dow represented a drop of 19.26 percent, just short of the 20 percent decline that defines a bear market. Another 0.74 percent would have meant that the great bull market of the 1990s would be declared officially over. Trading volumes on August 27 and August 31 were the second and third highest in history, respectively, showing that everybody was jumping ship.

September 1, 1998 — Once again the market immediately rebounded (Alan Greenspan helped by letting it be known he was going to address the key problems affecting the market). The day after its near-record loss, the

Dow put up a near-record gain. The Dow gained 288.36 points, then the second biggest gain ever (it now ranks seventh). Investors poured back into the market, driving the NYSE volume to a then all-time high of 1.216 billion shares. The Nasdaq had its second highest volume day, edging out the NYSE with a volume of 1.259 billion shares. It was then only the second time both markets had gone over a billion shares (the first time was during the 10/28/1997 rebound). Now Greenspan needed to take some affirmative steps to support the rebound.

During the turmoil of September, Greenspan took two big steps. First the Federal Reserve cut interest rates by one-quarter percentage point. Some would have liked a bigger cut, but at least it was a decrease — the first reduction since January of 1996. Also, the Fed arranged a bailout of a well-known hedge fund, Long-Term Capital Management. It was considered to be too big to fail because it would have taken other companies with it, and greatly upset an already fragile market.

Greatly overextended in its highly leveraged trading accounts, the company was essentially insolvent and ready for bankruptcy. Many so-called savvy Wall Street investors were shocked by the news because the fund was run by self-proclaimed geniuses who learned their trade in the treasury bond scandals of the 1990s. They claimed to use the most sophisticated risk management techniques presently available, and they had convinced themselves and their Wall Street admirers that their ship was unsinkable. They couldn't have been very smart if they thought they had discovered a system in which they couldn't lose. At any rate, their can't-lose system ended up like all such other systems — it lost, hugely.

Uncle Alan showed how ready he was to prop up the market by getting the fund's lenders and various Wall Street bankers and brokers to put up the $3.5 billion to bail out the geniuses. The consortium greatly limited what steps the fund could take until their debts were paid off.

September 8, 1998 — One week later the markets had enough assurance that Uncle Alan would come through that the Dow gained 380.53 points, then the biggest one day point gain ever (it still ranks second behind the 499.19 gain the Dow posted when it was over 10,000 points in March of 2000). But for the rest of September and into October, 1998, the Dow began a series of ups and downs as rumors continued running about the problems of hedge funds and derivatives investors.

October 16, 1998 — The Dow stepped forward with a gain of 330.58 points on this day, then the third (and still the fourth) biggest one day gain in history. The Dow had stood at 8,523.35 on 8/26/1998, the night before its big loss on 8/27/1998. After its big gain today, the Dow stood at 8,299.36, a drop of only 2.6 percent after its series of gains and losses since 8/27/1998. The Dow was now ready to resume its march upwards. Greenspan had done it again.

October 22, 1998 — Daimler-Chrysler became the first international corporation to list its ordinary shares directly on the NYSE.

December 22, 1998 — With volumes heading for a billion shares a day on a regular basis, the NYSE reached a preliminary agreement to build a new trading facility across the street (Broad Street) from its present facilities.

January 6, 1999 — The Dow closed over 9,500 for the first time. The small panic of August and September 1998 now lay forgotten in its rear view mirror.

January 29, 1999 — The Nasdaq more than kept pace with the Dow as it closed over 2,500 for the first time.

March 29, 1999 — In a startling series of rapid changes for an average now as high as the Dow, the Dow closed over 10,000 for the first time less than three months after it passed 9,500.

April 21, 1999 — Three weeks after reaching 10,000, the Dow went right over the 10,500 mark.

May 3, 1999 — Another 12 days took the Dow over 11,000. But more rational minds were beginning to make themselves felt. The Dow would not go over 11,500 for another eight months, and then the party would end.

August 23, 1999 — Another investor wanted in at any price. A seat was sold on the NYSE for a record price of $2.65 million.

November 1, 1999 — Among other changes, the Dow Jones Industrial Average added Microsoft and Intel to its list of 30 stocks. Both of these stocks were listed on the Nasdaq (the Nasdaq was now a big-time market in every possible way), but not on the NYSE. It was the first time in its history of 103 years that the Dow included stocks not listed on the NYSE. It was another step in the blurring of the differences between the two most significant indexes. For the record, the 30 stocks that made up the Dow as of this date were: Allied Signal, Aluminum Company of America (Aloca), American Express, AT&T, Boeing, Caterpillar, Citigroup, Coca Cola,

DuPont, Eastman Kodak, Exxon, General Electric, General Motors, Hewlett Packard, Home Depot, IBM, Intel, International Paper, Johnson & Johnson, McDonalds, Merck, Microsoft, Minnesota Mining and Manufacturing, J.P. Morgan, Philip Morris, Procter & Gamble, SBC Communications, United Technologies, Wal-Mart, and Walt Disney.

November 3, 1999— The Nasdaq picked up the baton for the insane rush upwards while the Dow took a nap. The Nasdaq closed over 3,000 for first time, just nine months after it crossed 2,500. The gain of 20 percent in nine months extrapolated to a gain of 27 percent per year.

December 3, 1999— To show off a little, the Nasdaq took only one month to go from 3,000 and close over 3,500 for the first time. This gain of 17 percent in one month extrapolated to madness.

December 29, 1999— To prove it was no fluke, the Nasdaq now added another 500 points in less than one month as it closed over 4,000 for first time. Over the cheering, the scent of a big, big bubble was unmistakable. In the 12 months between 1/6/1999 and 1/7/2000, the Dow would go from 9,500 to 11,500, an increase of 21 percent in one year. Good, but very far from the best ever (it went up 82 percent, for example, in 1915, and the tenth best year was 34 percent in 1958). Certainly no sign of a bubble here.

However, in the 11.3 months from 1/19/1999 to 12/29/1999, the Nasdaq went from 2,500 to 4,000, an increase of 60 percent in 11.3 months. This extrapolated to a yearly rate of 70 percent. More ominous, the Nasdaq went from 3,000 to 4,000 in the 56 days between 11/3/1999 and 12/29/1999. This was an increase of 33 percent in just under two months. The Nasdaq was climbing over 16 percent a month, a rate which if maintained over a full 12 months would produce an increase of six times at the end of the year. Any sensible person should already have begun to run for cover. But the Nasdaq bubble was not done growing, proving that P.T. Barnum was right.

December 31, 1999— The Dow closed the year and the decade at 11,497.12. It had closed the 1980s at 2,753.2. Thus, for the 1990s, the Dow had increased by nearly 4.2 times, or +320 percent. It was the best decade ever for the Dow. But the prior decade record holder was the 1950s at +240 percent (the 1980s came in at +230 percent). Thus, the 1990s were not far out of proportion to previous good decades. Once again, there was no sign of a Dow bubble being built in the 1990s.

January 7, 2000— The Dow climbed up only three more points as the new year (considered by most people to be a new century) opened, closing over 11,500 for the first time in the process.

January 14, 2000— The Dow finally reached its mountain top today. It closed at 11,722.98, its all-time record high. This brought the bull market of the 1990s to a close in the sense that this peak has not yet been surpassed (near the end of August, 2001, the Dow was trading in the 10,200 range). Calling what has happened since a bear market depends on the somewhat esoteric definition used. The Dow was 16 percent below its peak in March of 2000, and it was down a rounded 20 percent in March of 2001, its two lowest points in the 19 months between January 2000 and mid-August 2001. But it certainly did not "crash."

Measuring the bull market from the low at the beginning to its peak, the bull market of the 1990s was both the biggest and longest in history. The Dow was at 2,365.10 when the bull market of the 1990s began on October 11, 1990. It peaked nine years and three months later on this date, showing a gain of 4.957 times or +395.7 percent. The next biggest bull markets were those that preceded the big crashes in 1929 and 1987. The bull market of the 1920s ran from 1923 to 1929, with a gain of 344.5 percent. The bull market of the 1980s ran from 1982 to 1987, with a gain of 250.4 percent. The bull market of the 1990s was much longer and notably bigger than the prior two, and, at least in terms of the Dow, it was not followed by a crash.

After peaking today, the Dow drifted back under 11,000 at the end of January. It closed the month at 10,940.53, but it was still higher than the low for the month when it touched 10,738.87

February 17, 2000— As the Dow regained its senses to some degree, the Nasdaq continued rising, closing above 4,500 for the first time on this day. This marked a gain of 12.5 percent in the 50 days since it passed 4,000 on 12/29/2000. The rate of growth of the big bubble was slowing to somewhat less ridiculous levels, but the bubble would get one more blast of air before it burst in three weeks.

February 29, 2000— The Dow closed February at 10,128.31, after falling through the 10,000 mark during the month, when it got down to 9,862.12. It lost 812.22 points for the month, but this would be its biggest monthly loss for the full year of 2000. Its descent would continue to be gentle.

March 7, 2000— The Dow hit a low of 9,796.03 on March 7, but this turned out to be its lowest close for the year. The Dow was now 16.4 percent lower than its record close on January. But a difference of 16.4 percent between the high of a year and the low for a year is hardly worth mentioning in the history of the Dow. The Dow had essentially had its "crash" for 2000. The rest of the year it would float generally in the mid-10,000s, doing what all markets do best, fluctuating. But it would fluctuate in a relatively narrow range on a percentage basis.

March 9, 2000—The Nasdaq closed above 5,000. This was an increase of 11.1 percent in only 21 days, a rate of about 16 percent per month. The Nasdaq bubble was now continuing to expand at an insane rate. But the bubble blowers were near exhaustion.

March 10, 2000—On the next day, a Friday, the Nasdaq bubble grew to its largest size, as the Nasdaq peaked at 5,132. The Nasdaq would now descend to 1,638.8 in 13 months. If you wonder how this could happen, consider the fact that, as we will describe in the 2001 milestones, only 1.5 percent of all analysts would use the dreaded word "sell" in their recommendations to their starry-eyed customers as the Nasdaq fell from its high to its low. All the way down the huge drop of 68 percent, so-called experts would say the stocks that made up the Nasdaq were excellent buys, just as they had been saying all along (if these analysts had a theme song, it would have to be "I'm forever blowing bubbles..."). Many of these "objective" analysts increased their income by being a shill for the stocks. But the greedy customers who mindlessly followed the bogus recommendations of the analysts cannot escape without carrying a good share of the blame.

March 4, 2000—As has happened so often, investors took the weekend to wonder if the market was getting ready to tank. They were still thinking it over on Monday, but on this Tuesday, they decided to jump. The Nasdaq suffered what was then the second biggest point loss in its history, 200.61 points. Ironically, before today, what was then the biggest point loss had come on January 4, 2000 (229.46 points) as the Nasdaq was zig-zagging its way up to its March all-time high. These two losses would be pushed into fifth and sixth place, respectively, once the Nasdaq starting recording more big losses in April 2000, now only two weeks in the future.

March 16, 2000—The Dow gained 499.19 points for its largest point gain in history. The Dow closed the day at 10,630.60, so its gain represented only 4.93 percent, a very small percentage for such a large point gain, but small percentages should be expected for a Dow well over 10,000. The Dow reached a high of 11,119.86 during the month, only 5.1 percent below its all-time high in January. It just kept rolling along with the tide.

March 20, 2000—The Nasdaq lost another 188.13 points today, now the tenth highest point loss for the Nasdaq.

March 29, 2000— The Nasdaq followed up with a loss of another 189.22 points, presently its ninth highest point loss in history. The Nasdaq kept bouncing around as sellers wanted to sell to keep their gains, but then jumped right back in when there was an upturn because they didn't want to miss out on a possible rebound. So far in its recent history the Nasdaq has always come back to grow higher, and the "experts" are still pushing Nasdaq stocks as good buys.

The result was that while the three big losing days in March added up to a total loss of 578 points in just the three days, the ups and downs of the rest of the month washed each other out. The Nasdaq closed the month just over 4,500, as the net loss to date from the all-time high almost exactly equals the 578 points due to just the three big losses. This was a loss of "only" 11.3 percent.

April 3, 2000— The first trading day of April produced what was then the biggest point loss in Nasdaq history, a drop of 349.15 points. This loss would be surpassed in only 11 days, but 4/3/2000 still ranks as the second biggest loss ever for the Nasdaq. With the Nasdaq now appearing in danger of dropping below 4,000, its investors were really beginning to squirm.

April 10, 2000— In the rest of the week following 4/3/2000, the Nasdaq recovered somewhat from its 4/3/2000 dip, but on this (yet another) Monday, the Nasdaq lost another 258.25 points, still the fourth biggest loss in Nasdaq history.

April 12, 2000— Two days later, on Wednesday, the Nasdaq took a hit of 286.27 points, still the third biggest loss in its history.

April 14, 2000— This day, a Friday, the Nasdaq ended a really ugly week by registering its all-time highest loss of 355.49 points. This daily loss has not been surpassed to date, although there were lots of losses yet to come. At the end of this day, the Nasdaq stood at just over 3,300 (a loss of 1,800 points or 35 percent from its all-time high just one month earlier). No one knew that the Nasdaq still had another 1,700 points to go before it would hit an apparent bottom of 1,638.8, almost exactly one year later. In a sense today, April 14, 2000, is a halfway point in the Nasdaq crash. It had lost 1,800 points from its high, and would lose another 1,700 before it stopped falling.

The Nasdaq would begin a big rally after this weekend passed. The top eight of its ten biggest point gains would take place between this date and October of this year. It would bounce constantly up and down, but the longed-for rebound would not happen.

The Nasdaq loss of 355.49 points on this day represented a percentage loss of 9.67 percent, still the second biggest percentage loss in Nasdaq history. Only the crash of 10/19/1987, which produced a loss of 11.35 percent, ranks higher. The Nasdaq was below 500 in 1987, making it easier to establish a new percentage loss than now, when the Nasdaq was near 3,500. But the Nasdaq would still establish eight of its ten highest percentage gains between this date and October, matching the big point gains coming up, as noted above.

One way to consider the big Nasdaq gains (and subsequent losses) that followed is to say that it is a very resilient index. Another way to consider the big bounces is that a lot of investors couldn't face reality and were determined to catch the (mythical) Nasdaq rebound that was sure to come. It was as if a group of tourists were determined to force their way onto a famous tour ship just before it lost its steerage and went over the waterfall downriver. The investors anxious to catch the Nasdaq "bounce" after it lost 35 percent to date from its all-time high got to ride the Nasdaq all the way down to its total loss of 68 percent (or more).

While everyone was mesmerized by the plunging Nasdaq, on this day the Dow also had its all-time record point loss (not a good day for any investor). The Dow dropped 617.78 points (5.66 percent) and closed this day at 10,305.77 (its low for the month). The percentage loss was nowhere near a record, and in spite of the big one day point loss, the Dow went on to close April at 10,733.99, only 12 percent below its all-time high set in January. The Dow kept cruising while staying away from those infamous waterfalls.

April 16, 2000— The *Fortune* magazine issue of April 17, 2000, in circulation on this day, contained some letters commenting on the issue of March 20, 2000, which published an article addressing some of the nonsense taking place on the Nasdaq market relative to the marketing and selling of Internet companies. The article was called "Doing Business the Dot-Com Way." Some of these letters, written in March after the article appeared in the March 20 issue, address well the disaster taking place in the Nasdaq in April. It is ironic to note that the article was written just before the Nasdaq peaked and started to collapse.

One letter writer pointed out that when he questioned the viability of some of the proposed Internet companies, he was told that he was unlearned in the new way of doing business. Venture capitalists only had to hit on one or two of each seven startups to make their killing. The failures were shrugged off. The letter finished by saying the new breed had "unwisely dismissed profitability as an out-of-date objective, and failed to learn that there are responsibilities when one uses other people's money." The attitude made one believe that many new companies were created only to roll the dice to see if it would be one of the few that would make a profit for the underwriters, whether through profitable products or shady deals as an insider when the IPO (Initial Public Offering) was processed.

The situation might be seen as reminiscent of that in Iran in 1974, when hot competition for weapons programs for the Shah enabled every government or military official to take a piece of the action — "baksheesh" — at every step of the procurement process. In one case a weapons system was designed, a bid process was carried out, a contract was let, and the system was built, tested successfully, delivered in Iran (after much was paid to move it quickly through the queue awaiting entry), and moved to a warehouse in a remote outpost in the desert. There it sat, and may sit to this day. It had no real end use. The whole process took place just to let every official at every point collect his usual fee under the table. In the official view nothing really illegal took place. It was a competitively bid contract with a properly built end product, even though it existed just to be a cash cow.

One can wonder how many Internet companies were created in such a way. No one cared at the top level if they survived or not. Once the underwriting fee was collected, the IPO marketed with the usual insider profits (including those for the analysts pushing the stock and helping themselves to their share), and the stock price pushed as high as possible and then sold, seemingly no one cared if the company survived. Those who bought the stock on an analyst's recommendation and those who honestly tried to make a company succeed when it never had a chance were the only ones who got hurt.

Another letter in this issue of *Fortune* referred to a prior article about the "new" process of day trading. The letter pointed out that the process was not new at all; only the name and the technology were new. In the 1920s places called "bucket shops," meant to be a derogatory name, offered facilities where "underinformed, overleveraged investors could go to lose their money in the name of investing." The letter concluded that the only people who got rich then and now were the proprietors who catered "to people's greed." Perhaps it should be no surprise that the Nasdaq fell so far so fast.

April 17, 2000 — Investors who emptied their piggy banks over the weekend to catch the Nasadaq rebound that just had to come drove the Nasdaq up by 217.87 points on this Monday, giving the Nasdaq its seventh biggest point gain in history. A drive upward, if not the rebound, had started.

April 18, 2000 — Pleased with their work of the previous day, investors drove the Nasdaq up another 254.41 points, still its largest one-day point gain in history in spite of the gains posted while the Nasdaq rocketed upwards at the end of the 1990s. Gaining almost 500 points in two days pushed the Nasdaq back up towards 3,800.

April 25, 2000 — Today, only one week after its great back-to-back gained, the Nasdaq gains 228.75 points, its sixth biggest gain ever. However, all this gain did was to return the Nasdaq to its level of one week earlier, because the Nasdaq had lost a nearly equivalent amount of points in the week that just went by. The Nasdaq just couldn't get back to 4,000. Riding the Nasdaq is not for those who are prone to sea sickness.

May 30, 2000 — The Nasdaq spent the month of May oscillating between roughly 3,200 and 3,800. It was near the low end of that range when it started a furious rally on this date just as May was about to end. The Nasdaq gained 254.37 points, its second biggest gain ever, a miniscule 0.04 points behind the all-time record it set back on April 18th. Because it had been running near a lowly 3,200, the percentage gain of 7.94 percent on this day was its highest percentage gain ever. Investors wondered if this was the beginning of the long awaited rebound.

June 2, 2000 — After pausing for breath on Wednesday, May 31, the Nasdaq ended the week by booming upwards on the first two days of June, gaining 181.59 points on June 1, its eighth biggest gain ever, and gaining 230.88 points today, its fifth biggest gain ever. The Nasdaq was now over 3,800, and it would break back over 4,000 before the month was out. This would lead it into a summer of almost three identical months (July, August, and September), trading between a low of 3,700 and a high near 4,200. But after this pause of raised expectations, the Nasdaq would not continue its "rebound," but would start the long trek downwards again.

August 28, 2000 — While the Nasdaq continued to fluctuate, the NYSE on this date began trading in decimal increments for seven stocks in a pilot program. The plan was to have all NYSE stocks trading in decimal increments by 1/29/2001, thus ending the practice of trading in eighths, which had been going on for more than two centuries.

September 29, 2000 — The Dow closed at 10,650.92. This rounds off to 10,651, almost exactly equal to the 10,687 average closing that the Dow would post for the entire year of 2000. The Dow reached a high close of 11,310.64 during this month, its highest mark for the year except for the record of 11,722.98 it reached in January. Thus, as the last quarter of the year 2000 began, the Dow remained at an average closing mark that was only 8.8 percent below its all-time high.

October 13, 2000— Today represented a piece of good news for the Nasdaq. After drifting down to about 3,100 and appearing ready to fall under 3,000 for the first time in a year, on this day (Friday the 13th), the Nasdaq registered yet another bounce upwards, gaining 242.09 points (the fourth highest gain in its history) to climb back to 3,300.

October 19, 2000— After squandering most of what it gained the previous Friday, the Nasdaq rallied again, adding 247.04 points (its third biggest one day gain in its history) to end near 3,400. It still refused to fall through the 3,000 level that many analysts feared would lead to more sharp declines.

The analysts were right this time. The Nasdaq could not reverse its long decline from its high. In the middle of November, the Nasdaq finally would fall through the 3,000 level, ending the month near 2,600. In early December it would rally again to get back near 3,000, but then it would fall below 2,500 near the end of the year. This would put the Nasdaq down more than 50 percent from the high it reached in March. The elusive Nasdaq rebound was still nowhere to be found.

November 20, 2000— The new trading floor for the NYSE opened at 30 Broad Street, less than two years after the preliminary agreement was reached to build it (see entry for 12/22/1998). This trading floor added another 8,000 square feet to the NYSE supply. This addition showed how the need to keep adding trading floors gave the NYSE stock trading system a disadvantage compared to the electronic "floor" of the Nasdaq, even if made the NYSE more of an open auction system than the Nasdaq. Certainly it also showed that building a system to duplicate the NYSE appeared prohibitively expensive.

December 21, 2000— The NYSE Direct+, an automatic execution service, was launched as a pilot program. The NYSE continued to be a formidable competitor for the so-called "Stock Market of the Future" as represented by the Nasdaq.

December 31, 2000— The Dow closed the year 2000 at 10,786.85, down only 7.98 percent from its all-time high set on 1/14/2000. The Dow closed 1999 at 11,490.12, meaning that, for the entire year of 2000, the Dow lost only 6.1 percent. This was additional evidence that only the Nasdaq had a "crash" in 2000. On a year-to-year basis, the Dow did not even meet the 10 percent loss criteria often used to define a "correction."

January 3, 2001— Alan Greenspan and the Fed surprised everyone by announcing an interest rate cut of one-half point. It would turn out to be the first of seven cuts in the first eight months of 2001. These cuts would take 3.00 percentage points off the Fed rate in those eight months. The Fed would soon be suspected of trying to pump up the stock market rather than balancing the strength of the economy versus inflation. The Japanese could not pump up their decade-long crash in their stock market even with zero interest rates (and for a short time rates that were technically negative; i.e. the banks were paying customers to borrow money). Such bribes only made things worse, but as always every country has to learn everything for themselves. No one ever seems to learn anything from other people's mistakes.

January 4, 2001— The NYSE celebrated the rate cut by setting an all-time volume record as it went over two billion shares for the first time. The final count was exactly 2,129,445,637 shares traded. This broke the record of 1.56 billion shares traded on 12/15/2000, just 15 days earlier. The NYSE broke all of its prior volume records in 2000, a year when the NYSE, as noted earlier in the book, averaged over one billion shares traded daily. The year 2000 was the first year the NYSE ever averaged more than one billion shares traded every day, but it certainly won't be the last. You can be sure the Nasdaq will keep pace with, or generally even lead, the NYSE in volume.

January 29, 2001— The NYSE met its goal of trading all listed issues in decimals by this date (see entry for 8/28/2000). The Nasdaq would also switch to all decimal pricing.

January 31, 2001— The Nasdaq dipped below 2,300 early in the new year, then rallied once more to get back to 2,800 before January ended. It dipped a little at the end of the month, popped back to 2,800 as February started, and then began a new decline that would take it almost straight down for the next two months.

March 30, 2001— The Dow closed the last trading day in March at 9,800, after dipping to 9,400 in the middle of the month. The dip to 9,400 was the first time the Dow had been below 9,500 since it first passed 9,500 on the way up on January 6, 1999. The 9,400 level was 20 percent below the 11,723 record set by the Dow on 1/14/2000, the furthest the Dow has gotten below its record of 1/14/2000 through late August 2001. But the Dow almost made it back to 10,000 before March was over, then dipped back down to 9,500 in early April in sympathy with the Nasdaq. The Nasdaq fell to 1,638.8 in early April, its low so far since it peaked in March of 2000. The Dow quickly bounced back over 10,000 by the middle of April and stayed above 10,000 the rest of the time (through late August 2001).

April 17, 2001— The Nasdaq closed below 2,000 on this date, although it was now climbing steadily upward from its post-crash low of 1,638.8 early in the month. It would climb above 2,000 the next day, and today would be the last day the Nasdaq spent below 2,000 for the next two months.

In summary, after falling through 2,000 in March 2001, the Nasdaq reached 1,638 in early April. Nasdaq followers hoped that 1,638 would mark the bottom of the slide that started 13 months earlier, when the Nasdaq peaked at 5,132 on March 10, 2000. If 1,638 does turn out to be the bottom of the Nasdaq crash, the Nasdaq will have fallen by 68 percent from its peak. The last time the Nasdaq was in the 1,600s was in the fall of 1998. It first passed 1,600 in mid-1997, nearly four years before its 1,638.8 low. The middle of 1997 now seemed a very long time ago for Nasdaq followers. If one rode the Nasdaq all the way up and all the way down, the Nasdaq essentially had gone nowhere for four years.

May 21, 2001— On this merry Monday in May, the Dow closed just below 11,340, only 3.3 percent below its record high set in January of 2000. It was the highest point the Dow would reach in the first eight months of the year 2001, but it was clear evidence that the Dow was not in any form of a post-crash mode. Except for the general overall market dip at the end of March and early April of this year (when the Nasdaq fell to its post-crash low), the Dow stayed in a range between 10,200 and 11,000 from November of 2000 to August of 2001.

June 18, 2001— After getting over 2,000 in mid-April, the Nasdaq stayed in a range between 2,000 and 2,300 for two months, apparently stabilizing at this level. But on this date, the Nasdaq dipped below 2,000 again. It only fell to 1,989, but its most faithful followers had thought values below 2,000 were in the past. The Nasdaq, as always, bounced back from this dip, but after struggling above 2,150 by the end of this month, it would fall perilously close to 1,950 during two separate dips in July. As of late August 2001, the Nasdaq had fallen back into the 1,800s again, its lowest level in over four months. There was no sign of the fabled rebound (in spite of Greenspan's seven rate cuts).

June 20, 2001— As the dust began to settle on the collapse of the Nasdaq and the full extent of the losses now seemed clear, the inevitable questions of "what happened" were now in full circulation. The *Los Angeles Times* on this date carried an article reviewing the effect of stock recommendations by analysts on the profits realized by investors. The article stated frankly that while most professionals considered such information worthless, the influx of new investors into the bull market of the 1990s produced a new result because many of these new (naive) investors gave more credence to such nonsense.

Studies were being made in preparation for congressional hearings, led by Representative Richard H. Baker, which were to begin on June 21, 2001. The focus would be on the potential conflicts of interest for analysts who make such recommendations. Everyone on Wall Street was aware such analysts were loath to say anything bad about a stock in which they, or their company, or both, had a financial interest. Baker himself said he was aware of the "grade inflation" analysts gave to such stocks, saying that when the analyst gave the stock a rating of "hold," he really meant "get out now." These hearings would trigger a flood of articles and comments and even subsequent lawsuits, which we will cover briefly in the following pages.

One study, released before the hearings, showed that over 70 percent of analysts' recommendations were "strong buy" or "buy" as the Nasdaq neared its peak in February of 2000. Almost 30 percent were "hold" or "neutral." Less than 1 percent said "underperform" or "sell."

The revealing statistic is that these percentages stayed almost exactly the same in May and December of 2000 as the Nasdaq collapsed. Even as late as June 2001, while the collapse continued, as noted above, the recommendations were nearly unchanged, with only 1.2 percent suggesting the stock was in the "underperform" or "sell" categories. The percentages in these categories ranged from 0.7 percent in February 2000, just before the peak, to 0.8 percent in May 2000, as the collapse was rolling, to 1.0 percent in December 2000, as the collapse was grinding on, and to 1.2 percent in June 2000 as noted above. Analysts could not bring themselves to utter the word "sell" for fear of upsetting the companies who were providing their income.

Of course, one could ask why an investor would stand starry-eyed looking at the analyst while the world collapsed around them. It takes two to make a fraudulent process succeed.

June 25, 2001—Now that the "what happened" floodgates were opened, new revelations and accusations came from everywhere. In the issue of *Time* dated 6/25/2001, columnist Daniel Kadlec managed to mention the names of Ivan Boesky, Michael Milken, the movie *Wall Street* ("greed is good"), and Mary Meeker (the all-star Internet analyst for Morgan Stanley), among others, all in the first nine sentences. Kadlec later added Henry Blodgett, star Internet analyst for Merrill Lynch, and essentially pointed out that all of these people were guilty of the same thing—using their special positions to shear the public sheep who came running as fast as they could to enrich themselves from the Nasdaq bubble.

It is pointed out that Meeker and Blodgett made $15 million each by touting stocks for which they got huge fees when their companies underwrote the IPOs (Initial Public Offering) of new companies, and everyone got to share in the pots of money made when insiders bought IPOs at sweetheart prices and sold them later to the "bigger idiots" running at full speed into the bubble.

June 27, 2001— Alan Greenspan cut interest rates another one-quarter percent to bring the total cuts for the first six months of the year to two and three-quarters percent. The rate was now 3.75 percent, and the reductions were the steepest and the swiftest by the Fed since 1982. It almost appeared that Greenspan was trying to say he was sorry for the rate increases during 2000 that were meant to moderate the ever surging markets, that he now thought that they were a big mistake, and that he wanted to make up for the mistake as soon as possible. Questions were being asked seriously as to whether Greenspan was worried about the economy, as he should be, or worried about bringing the good old days back to the stock markets, which is not his job.

July 2, 2001— In a touch of perhaps unrecognized irony, *Time* columnist Kadlec came back to tout technology stocks. Once again he trotted out the argument about having an outlook of 25 or 50 years, not mentioning what to do if one didn't have that many years left.

At least he admitted his prior bad advice to real analysts like Warren Buffet and Peter Lynch, probably the two most famous market advisors in the country, to get with the movement to technology. He criticized Lynch, who couldn't operate a PC, and Buffet, who wouldn't touch a PC stock, as being technophobic. Considering Kadlec offered his criticism just five months before the Nasdaq collapsed, he admitted he often had crow for dinner. Kadlec's present column showed how hard it was to avoid being seduced by the technology bubble. Everyone has the right to dream about striking it rich.

July 3, 2001— The NASD, operator of the Nasdaq, said in an article that it wanted the analysts to offer full disclosure. It wanted to restore the public's faith in Wall Street. That's what was said after the 1929 crash and the 1987 crash. But the nice words didn't change the fact that the cycle continues. As markets grow, the greed of the "professionals" seduces them into moving to unethical and then illegal behavior to keep the pot boiling and the income flowing. That gets a bubble going, and in comes the public looking for some of that "easy money." What they get is fleeced, and the bubble pops.

Charles Dow was right when he editorialized in 1899 that the growing mixing of professionals and public was a bad thing, because "the public" was most interested in short term profits. Actually the pros and the public have been well served by the growth of the public participation in the stock market during the past century. The country as a whole and the individuals holding stocks through their mutual funds, 401(k) plans, and the like have been a huge success. But when a bubble forms and then pops, lots of people lose in the short run. And the cause is always the same. There is no effective preventative for greed.

July 8, 2001 — In its Sunday business section, the *Los Angeles Times* ran a long article asking if perhaps Greenspan "has lost his Midas touch" or if he was given "too much credit" for the good days. Greenspan was accused of contributing to the market bubble by keeping rates too low in 1998 and early 1999, and causing the stall in the market by raising rates too much in the balance of 1999 and early 2000. But since there were really two different markets going on, at least after 1998, it's hard to blame the Nasdaq crash on Greenspan.

There was no complaint in the article about the rapid and large cuts in 2001, but now there was concern that the Fed's interest cutting tool was not such a magic tool, after all. If the real tool had been faith that Uncle Alan could make everything all right, that tool wouldn't work either now that the crash took place and the Nasdaq came tumbling down.

July 9, 2001 — In the *New Yorker* magazine published for this date, Christopher Buckley offered a new set of stock market axioms for the "Shouts and Murmurs" part of the magazine. Probably the most applicable in the ongoing "come clean" atmosphere was his definition of "downside." In his view, a downside was "a term preferred by brokers to describe a financial calamity. Considered less alarming to a client's ear than loss, crater, nosedive, tank, flameout, or bankruptcy."

July 10, 2001 — Merrill Lynch announced that it planned to ban its analysts from owning stock in the companies they covered. This was intended to answer critics who said that analysts couldn't hope to be objective about their recommendations for a stock they owned or from which they derived big bonuses for bringing the company into their brokerage house to generate underwriting fees. Critics pointed out that this was not just speculation. Study after study showed that analysts continued to tout their stocks even after they collapsed in the market.

July 13, 2001 — Michael Kinsley, syndicated columnist and occasional TV talk show star, had excerpts from one of his columns published in the

Los Angeles Times on this date. He was addressing the issue of whether the advice of analysts was corrupted by various conflicts of interest. He cynically pointed out that this question should be just as viable when stocks are going up, but nobody really cares until stocks go down (and people lose money). He referenced a cover story in *Fortune* in May about Internet star analyst Mary Meeker. She is quoted as saying that she was not "really aggressive on the downside" about companies her own company brought to market, and that she had continually puffed up some stocks relentlessly even as the stocks went into the toilet. Perhaps the saddest part was that she did not appear to see any "wrongdoing" in what she was doing. So it goes.

July 19, 2001— In an article published in the *Los Angeles Times* about Alan Greenspan's recent semiannual report to the House Financial Services Committee, it was pointed out that Greenspan's key word was patience. It takes six months for cuts to produce an effect in the economy, so we must wait a little longer for results. Stocks fell a little on all fronts. The Dow maintained its 10,500 range, and the Nasdaq hung in just below 2,000.

July 20, 2001— An article was published by the *Los Angeles Times* that could be an ominous sign for brokerage houses everywhere. Merrill Lynch announced that it had agreed to pay $400,000 to settle a case with an investor who claimed that he had lost money by "following the allegedly tainted recommendation" of Merrill analyst Henry Blodgett.

Other brokerage houses were concerned because Lynch settled the case quickly, and in the discovery phase, supposedly to avoid having to turn over Blodgett's files, which could leave Lynch vulnerable on other cases. Some lawyers said this date might be a milestone in stock market history in unleashing a flood of similar lawsuits.

July 23, 2001— In Tokyo, the Nikkei index fell to its lowest level in 16 years, hitting 11,609.63. The Japanese stock market peaked near 39,000 in 1989. It had fallen steadily since the bubble burst and was still reaching new lows. The decline from its peak was now 70 percent, and the decline had stretched out over 12 years. It had not been as low as it was today since 1985, when it was climbing to its peak and the Japanese economy was the wonder of the world.

July 24, 2001— The results of a study announced today in the *Los Angeles Times* said that a new SEC rule announced in October 2000 was not hurting the stock market as Wall Streeters had said it would. The rule required companies leaking sensitive information to selected brokerage firms and investors to make it public at the same time. Claims that the rule would make the market more volatile because companies would hesitate to release such information for fear of breaking the rule were found not to be true. The study found, on the contrary, that the rule resulted in more information being released, and, further, no difference in volatility was discovered. Thus, the rule could stand, constituting another step, however small, towards "full disclosure."

July 31, 2001— A survey of stock analysts released today by the SEC showed that 28 percent of the analysts had bought shares of stock at low prices in so-called private placements (that are unavailable to the public) before they told investors that their "research" indicated that these stocks were good buys. In three cases (more than 5 percent), the analysts even sold their shares while still recommending that the public buy them. The analysts made from $100,000 to $3.5 million in the process.

The survey concentrated on nine brokerage firms that underwrote IPOs, especially those of high technology companies. As a final grace note, the survey found that even in the special cases where analysts agreed to hold the shares for a specified time before dumping them, 27 percent sold the shares within a week after the specified time. The urge clearly was to take the money and run.

One could say that the SEC had found a "smoking gun," but the results surprised absolutely no one. Big brokerage houses stated that now that they knew about these terrible practices, they certainly would take steps to fix them. They didn't say when.

August 1, 2001— Today two lawsuits were filed against Mary Meeker, the "Queen of the Internet" (to go along with "King Henry" Blodgett of Merrill Lynch — see entry for 7/20/2001). The lawsuits claimed Meeker specifically pumped up the stocks of EBay and Amazon.com to get the companies to use her employer, Morgan Stanley, as their investment banker. This would create huge bonuses for Meeker. The suits sought class action status, which could greatly increase the damages to be paid if the suits were successful (a companion suit citing Meeker's biased work on AOL Time Warner was filed six days later). It appeared that, in future days, the King and the Queen were likely to see a field full of chickens coming home to roost.

August 3, 2001— An arbitrator ruled that one of the largest day trading firms in the nation, All-Tech Direct, had to pay $456,000 to cover losses suffered by four investors who claimed they were duped into believing they could make "easy money" by day trading. The arbitration panel worked for the NASD as part of the self-policing role the NASD performed for the

Nasdaq. The award would not entirely cover the losses suffered by the investors. All-Tech claimed the investors were at fault because they held stock overnight rather than selling it the same day as All-Tech advised. It was not the first rap on the knuckles for All-Tech. In June 2001, the NASD fined the company $475,000 for misleading advertisements about the risks of day trading. The advertisements were directed towards investors in an attempt to get them to try day trading. Unfortunately, "misleading" investors is all too easy to do.

August 7, 2001— Mark Jakob, an Internet investor who was trying to avoid personal losses suffered as a result of selling short, was sentenced to 4 years in prison for issuing a fake news release. Jakob claimed remorse but pointed out that he was bothered by the fact that the financial markets are "so fragile." He said that if others tried to do on a wide scale basis what he had done, it "could be disastrous."

On August 24, 2000, Jakob had issued a false news release saying that his target company, Emulex, was in serious trouble because its earnings were being restated, its chief executive had quit, and the SEC was investigating. Jakob used a community college computer to issue the release, and it was picked up by various media outlets the next morning without any questions being asked. The resulting panic in Emulex stock cost investors an estimated $110 million. Jakob himself made $241,000 in new profit and avoided a loss of $97,000 on his short sales that were his incentive for issuing the false release. His whole package of gain was seized, and he was fined $102,642 as well in an attempt to provide some restitution to investors.

But Jakob's warning was well meant. Yelling "fire" in a crowded theater cannot hold a candle to the panic caused in the Internet market when someone shouts the bubble is bursting.

August 13, 2001— In the issue of *Time* bearing this date, Daniel Kadlec gave "equal time" to the other side of the Nasdaq crash — poor choices by investors who were so uninformed that it cannot be said they should have known better. They did not know anything, and they should not have owned many of the "high tech" stocks in the first place. The offenses of the likes of Mary Meeker and Henry Blodgett have been held up to thorough scrutiny and lawsuits filed accordingly.

But no one has held up to scrutiny the offenses of the investors (the "bigger idiots" as I have called them). Kadlec proposed that the government should fund a Department of Pathetic Investors (to be known as DOPI) to look into the actions of investors who threw their money into a market they had no hope of understanding. He quotes cases of investors lying and cheating to get accounts permitting them to play in the marketplace, doing anything to get around the few restrictions brokerage houses do try to enforce to keep "unqualified" investors out of markets they have neither the assets or knowledge to enter.

In an article published in the *Los Angeles Times* the same weekend *Time* was being distributed, it was pointed out that no one should expect any significant changes in the IPO process. The professionals (investment banks, brokerages, and even the companies going public) like the system just fine. It is meant to service the professionals, and they get the major benefit from it. Read strictly, there is nothing illegal in the process, although some participants pay closer attention to professional ethics than others. The big losers are small (naive) investors who run after IPOs looking for some of that ever-popular "easy money." They chase new IPOs without much thought or understanding, and they lose big when IPOs crash and burn. In most cases they get just what they deserve.

This book has pointed out in detail how the same sequence of events happened in 1929, 1987, and 2000. The professionals couldn't resist cutting ethical and legal corners to keep the stock market bubble growing. The general public then jumped into markets they didn't understand in an attempt to get rich quick (or as Kadlec concludes, what they were really saying as they falsified documents to get into the market was "let me in on the easy money too").

The cycle has repeated through three big crashes in different markets and different eras. There is no reason to believe it will not repeat again, no matter how much the SEC and others tinker with the rules.

August 21, 2001— In another move to pump up the economy (stock market), Alan Greenspan and the Fed cut the Federal Funds rate another one-quarter percent. It was the seventh cut of the year. The rate had been reduced from 6.5 percent at the beginning of the year to 3.5 percent now. The rate was now at its lowest level since it was 3.0 percent in 1992-93. The Dow and Nasdaq "celebrated" by losing 146 points and 50 points respectively. The Dow was now at 10,174 and the Nasdaq at 1,831. The hoped-for rebound in the markets had yet to appear.

APPENDIX

1. BASIC INVESTMENT RISK

There are four basic investment risks. The first is asset risk. This is the risk that your investment will lose its value or even become worthless. If you buy a stock or bond in a company that goes bankrupt or is otherwise unable to pay its debts, your investment may be worthless. Buying an investment guaranteed by the federal government avoids this risk. If the federal government defaults, the country will be in trouble in a way that makes investing irrelevant. There are many government insured products available, such as CDs, treasury bills, notes, and bonds, and bonds issued by government agencies.

The second basic risk is market risk. Your investment may be fundamentally sound, but it may be worth less than you paid for it at the time you want to sell. Stocks in a market decline are a prime example. But even government bonds will lose value if interest rates increase, and, if you are forced to sell at such a time, you will lose money. For example, a $1,000 bond yielding six percent pays $60 interest annually. If you try to sell the bond when interest rates have increased to seven percent, a buyer will only be willing to pay about $857 for it so that the $60 annual interest represents a yield of seven percent on his investment. The government will pay $1,000 for the bond at maturity, but you have to hold it to maturity. This means you need to select bond maturities carefully.

The third risk is interest rate risk. You don't necessarily lose money because of this risk, but if you have planned your retirement based on a certain return on your investments and interest rates are lower than your planned rate when it comes time to reinvest, you will not meet your goals. You can avoid it with CDs or zero-coupon bonds that pay interest only at maturity. This means they will accumulate at your planned rate up to maturity. Again, careful planning is key.

The fourth risk is excess inflation risk. This is the risk that inflation rates will be so high that your assets will have far less purchasing power than planned. This risk is often exaggerated by people selling investments. The typical inflation rate of two to four percent will not ruin your retirement. The best protection against excess inflation is a stable financial system. If you invest only in the United States, you will stay in such a system, and you will also avoid currency exchange rate risk, which can be as bad as inflation risk. As long as the Federal Reserve Board is willing to increase interest rates as needed to avoid excess inflation (which is their basic job), and they ignore cries for lower rates just to help the stock market (which is not their job), inflation will be kept in check.

2. HIGH GROWTH FROM FIXED RATES

As I pointed out in the Introduction, fixed income investments can achieve very high rates of return if permitted to compound over a long period of time. This combines the magic of compound interest with tincture of time. Few investors are aware of the large increases that can result from CDs and bonds, because these investment vehicles are rarely advertised for returns over long periods of time. This leads to the perception that only the stock market can provide the high returns necessary to "beat inflation" and permit you to retire. But, as I pointed out in the Introduction, it's persistence and time that brings success in investing, not a genius for selecting stocks.

Rather than put my examples in tabular form, where they often are not fully understood, I'm simply going to list the returns available from a fixed price investment held for a long period of time. I think the straightforward statements of possible returns will have more impact than a table:

1. A $10,000 fixed rate investment compounding at a rate of 6.0 percent will grow to $57,000 in thirty years.

2. A $10,000 fixed rate investment compounding at a rate of 7.0 percent will grow to $76,000 in thirty years.

3. A $10,000 fixed rate investment compounding at a rate of 8.0 percent will grow to $101,000 in thirty years. If held for another five years, it will grow to $140,900.

4. A $10,000 fixed rate investment compounding at a rate of 9 percent will grow to $133,000 in thirty years. If it is held an additional five years, it will grow to $205,000.

The last example shows that a fixed rate investment compounding at 9% will grow by a factor of more than 20 in 35 years, and your balance will always show a gain at any point in the process. Few stocks can make such a claim.

You will not get these high rates by walking into a bank and asking for their best CD. You must use a stockbroker. Just as the "stock" market has many financial products available other than stocks, a "stockbroker" can provide many more financial products than stocks. I have worked with my present broker for the last 13 years, and he has never bought anything but bonds for my account. He is my guide into the incredibly complex marketplace available for financial products, and he can find the bonds that are guaranteed by the government to the extent I wish while offering the high yields I want. In this way, I take maximum advantage of the financial products marketplace.

I am retired and am 65 years old. Thus my future outlook extends only to another 20 years or so. Also, I am looking for current income from my investments, so I deal mainly in mortgage-backed securities backed by the full faith and credit of the U. S. Treasury. These are called "Ginnie Maes," and any broker can explain their advantages and disadvantages.

For long term investing for your retirement, I recommend zero-coupon bonds, as I noted in the introduction. Zero-coupon treasury bonds can be bought for periods as long as 30 years, and they are guaranteed by the government. The rates at which they can be bought vary like any investment, but once you have bought them, they compound at the same rate for their entire term. Thus, you are guaranteed that a specific amount will be available for your retirement, no matter what happens to the financial markets while you are waiting. If you buy them yearly, your initial rate will vary yearly, but that rate will be permanent until maturity.

Zero-coupon bonds do not pay out any interest, because it is accumulating as the bond matures. That is why they are called "zero-coupon" bonds. What actually happens is that you buy the bond at a big discount, and it grows to its full value at maturity. For example, a 6.1 percent bond with a maturity of 18 years would cost you $3300. In 18 years you would receive $10,000. When rates were near a peak in 1984, you could pay $303 for a short term bond that would pay you $1,000 in just 10 years. This is a rate of 12.5 percent. At this rate, the bond would double in value in less than 6 years. You would get a return of 16:1 in less than 24 years, compared to the rate of 16:1 in 36 years in the example in the Introduction. In 36 years, your return would be over 64:1. Those were the days.

Even though zero-coupon bonds do not pay you any interest in hand, the IRS takes the liberty of charging you income tax on the amount you could have received even if you did not actually receive it. The IRS has a habit of doing such things. Thus, zero-coupon bonds are best utilized in IRA-type accounts where taxes are not due until you actually withdraw the money.

The ins and outs of zero-coupon bonds are much too complex to be covered in a discussion of this type. They are not completely magical. You still have to carefully choose what interest rate and what term will fit your needs. What's available at any given time may not be acceptable to you. Again, careful planning is required. But I have taken extra time to outline their potential advantages so you will be inspired to find out more. Another advantage to keep in mind is that they will not keep you up at night worrying about the state of your investments.

3. LONG TERM STOCK MARKET DROPS

There have been a few long periods when stock markets fell or failed to grow. This phenomenon emphasizes the need for taking into account your age when you buy stocks. There are many announcements that say you should buy and hold stocks, and that also claim you should keep a good portion of your assets in stocks at retirement. I think this advice borders on the irresponsible.

It is true that on average, stocks have the best returns over long periods of time. But it is also true that a person can drown in a stream whose average depth is only 3 feet. If you step in at a deep place and can't swim, the average depth doesn't matter. Similarly, the good returns stocks give on average will not help you if you retire at the beginning of a period of a stock market decline. The fact that the market will finally come back after you are dead will not assist your enjoyment of your retirement. It is important to consider that stocks can fall for very long periods of time, even though they eventually come back.

The most infamous long term drop in the stock market in the United States happened in the crash of 1929. The Dow Jones Industrial Average peaked on September 3, 1929 at 381, and did not get back to 381 until 25 years later, in November of 1954. It fell to 41.22 in July of 1932, a drop of 89% from the peak. If you were counting on stocks in the Depression, you were in trouble. Cash was King in the depression.

The example in the Introduction should help you realize claims that 1929 "doesn't count" because it was so long ago are not true. In the Introduction, we talked about the market "growing" from 800 in early 1964 to 800 in the spring of 1980. If you retired in 1964, counting on the stock market, you were not helped by the fact that between 1980 and 2000, the market set record after record after record. It may have helped your descendants, but it did not help you. Zero-coupon bonds were a better choice for that period.

As noted also in the Introduction, the Japanese stock market peaked just under 39,000 at the end of 1989. The Japanese economy was considered to be competitive with any Western economy through the 1980s, and an investment in the Japanese stock market was considered the best one could make. In June 1995, the market was below 15,000, and today it often dips below 12,000. Anyone depending on the Japanese stock market since 1989 has not been a happy camper. It will likely be a long time in the future before the market returns to 39,000 or anything close to it. So be warned.

4. EVALUATING STOCKS

Stocks, like most pieces of property, are worth only what someone is willing to pay for them. In market declines, the sale price may be far below your cost (as discussed in #1). What I want to discuss here are methods that have been used to determine if the price of a stock is "reasonable" in relation to its "inherent" value. This will be helpful in considering whether or not to buy when a "great deal" is offered to you by some anxious salesman.

One of the standard methods of evaluating stocks is the price-to-earnings ratio (p/e ratio). In its simplest form, early in the century, this ratio tried to compare stocks to bonds, their main competitor then in the marketplace. Stocks usually paid half their earnings in dividends, and in those days dividends were key to buying stocks. Thus, if a stock earned $2.00 per share, it would pay $1.00 in dividends. One would want to earn at least five percent on a stock to stay ahead of the typical yield on high-class bonds, because stocks carried a higher market risk than bonds. Thus, the price of the stock should be no higher than $20 per share so that the investment yielded five percent with a dividend of $1. The result was a p/e ratio of 10 ($20 per share price compared to earnings of $2).

But other factors now need to be considered. If you are quite sure the company will continue to grow, and thus pay higher dividends in the future, you may be willing to pay a higher price today to capture those future dividends. Moreover, if the price of the stock goes up by $1 during the year, it will effectively double its $1 dividend in terms of the growth of your assets. Thus, you may be willing to pay twice as much for the stock, a p/e ratio of 20, and you will still feel you are making a sound investment. However, betting on the future increases your risk. Stocks generally command p/e ratios in the high teens, and when the Dow Jones index significantly exceeds a p/e ratio of 20, it's time to worry. The p/e ratio for many stocks exceeded 100 before the 1929 crash, and internet stocks climbed to infinity (zero earnings) before the 2000 crash.

A stock with a p/e ratio of infinity can be "reasonable" if it's a new company that puts its gross profits into research and development and marketing, leaving no net profits. If you (or your broker) are a student of balance sheets, you can conclude that this company is a good investment even if the southeast corner of the balance sheet shows zero net profit. If the operating profit and cash flow are good, the company may be sound. But, generally, p/e ratios higher than 20 are shouting "handle with care." That's just what you should do.

5. THE DOT.COM PHENOMENON

The dot.com phenomenon of the 1990s that resulted in the crash of the Nasdaq index in 2000, is one of the best (or worst, depending on your point of view) examples of blindly ignoring p/e ratios as discussed previously. It is also, I believe, one of the best/worst examples of the fact that stocks are sold, not bought. This means that considerable effort is made by an army of brokers to sell stocks to customers who have no business being in such investments.

The phrase "dot.com company" refers to businesses that sold products on the internet, and had names like Washingthedog.com. The ".com" part of the internet address gave its name to the entire phenomenon. In this case, we had companies whose p/e ratios were not only infinite, but companies that were not even close to earning a profit, gross or net. The stocks of these companies were sold on the basis that they would continually go up in price, and thus they should be bought for capital appreciation instead of old-fashioned things like dividends. Everyone was encouraged to get in on the ground floor, and many who did had the pleasure of watching the building collapse on top of them.

Stock exchanges have existed for at least 400 years, and so has the "greater fool" theory. This is a theory that says that it doesn't matter what outlandish price you pay for something, as long as there is a greater fool who will come along later and buy the item from you for more than you paid. In today's vernacular, we should use the term "bigger idiot" than "greater fool."

Even though people can now literally do their own trading on their own computers, many brokers bear a heavy responsibility for the dot-com crash. Even when Washingthedog.com was running out of dogs to wash and it was clear they were about to go under, brokers, many of whom were financially involved in these companies as a result of underwriting their initial public offerings (IPOs), continued to rate the companies a good buy. Even as the collapse continued, less than 1.5 percent of all broker ratings recommended selling dot.com stocks. The result was that the Nasdaq index fell from its high of just over 5,000 to under 2,000 in the year between early 2000 and 2001. This is more than a 60 percent drop, and it may be a long time before the Nasdaq gets back to 5,000. Right now, the Nasdaq has trouble staying above 2,000.

Of course, those who still believe the stock market magically offers something for nothing have to share a big part of the blame. As has often been said, if it sounds too good to be true, it probably isn't.

6. INDEXES

There are about nine basic indexes that are well known on Wall Street. The number is not precise because most of the basic indexes have within them several subindexes. I list them below roughly in order of popularity. The indexes are generally intended to indicate changes in the market, of course, but with the extensive development of options and various financial futures (both are essentially contracts to buy or sell assets within a specified period at a set price, although the details and tax treatment may differ substantially), the indexes have been put to uses for which they were not originally intended. I have not attempted to cover this aspect of indexes, because the number of new financial products grows exponentially.

Dow Jones Industrial Average

This is the most famous of the indexes. It started in 1896 as a true average of 12 industrial stocks. It now includes 30 stocks, which are revised as often as the Dow Jones company feels is necessary. It is no longer an exact average because the number by which the total prices of the 30 stocks is divided (the "divisor") has been changed as the stocks have changed and/or split. The changing of the divisor is intended to maintain the continuity of the average over time.

Since the method of calculating the average doesn't take into account the number of shares outstanding, higher-priced issues in the Dow have a greater influence than lower-priced issues. But this is not a key point. What is really true of nearly all of the indexes is that they are not really averages, but are indicators of changes in the stock market. It is not important to know how the average is derived. What is important is to know how it is changing.

Many analysts complain that having only 30 stocks in the Average cannot begin to be a good indicator of the general direction of the stock market, where more than 5,000 stocks are involved. But the Dow Jones company obviously has done a good job in picking the 30 representative stocks, because the Dow Jones average, since the 1920s, has generally correlated within one to two percent of the S&P 500, which as its name indicates, includes 500 stocks.

For that matter, over the last thirty years, the Dow Jones Average has correlated within one to two percent of the NYSE Composite, which includes all of the thousands of stocks traded on the NYSE.

So in spite of the naysayers, the Dow Jones' limited family of 30 stocks correlates very well with indexes that contain thousands of stocks. In addition, the Dow Jones Average existed for more than 60 years before the other averages began to be used in the marketplace. Thus, no average can match the Dow Jones for its length of service and continuity. Since it gets one year older every year, it is hard to imagine that any other index can replace the Dow Jones index in popularity.

The Dow Jones stock indexes include more than just the Dow Jones Industrials, but when people ask "How's the Dow?" it is the Industrials index they are referring to. There is also a *Dow Jones Transportation Average*, which is similar to the Dow Jones Industrials, except it consists of 20 selected stocks of large companies in the transportation industry. This index actually pre-dates the Dow Jones Industrial Averages by more than a decade. When it started, it consisted almost entirely of railroad stocks, which at the time, 1884, were the greatest growth stocks investors could imagine. As railroads fell out of favor, as nearly all stocks eventually do, the Railroad Average was renamed the Transportation Average in 1970 when it consisted of six airlines, three trucking companies, and the surviving 11 railroads. It has been subsequently revised, as all of the Dow Jones averages are, but it remains constant at 20 stocks.

The *Dow Jones Utility Average* is computed like its brethren, but as the name suggests, it consists of 15 utility companies. The Utility Average was started just before the crash in 1929. It started with 18 stocks, was increased to 20, and then cut to 15 in 1938. It has remained at 15 ever since. Even though it is named the Utility Average, it includes a mixture of electric generating utilities and natural gas utilities.

The *Dow Jones Composite Average*, as you might expect, includes the 30 industrial stocks, the 20 transportation stocks, and the 15 utility stocks of the other three averages. This means the Dow Jones Composite Average consists of 65 stocks. Only investors with specific interests in certain phases of the stock market pay much attention to the Composite Average, as well as the Transportation Average and the Utilities Average. Nearly all of the interest in the Dow Jones stock indexes is focused on the Dow Jones Industrials.

Nasdaq Composite Index

The next most popular index is the one based on the total stocks contained in the Nasdaq stock market. Since the Nasdaq has become the first or second biggest stock market in the world, depending on what you measure and when you measure it, it is natural that an index based on their market would be considered an important index. Also, because of the fact that the Nasdaq initially had a very heavy listing of stocks in the area of high technology (and still does), its index has reflected the very rapid growth of these stocks. Of course, its index also accurately reflected the bursting of the high tech bubble in 2001, and thus, the incredible growth rate that the index demonstrated in the 1990s was followed by an incredible decline between 2000 and 2001.

The Nasdaq, as usual, has a variety of indexes that investors can use. It has an index for its top 100 companies, and it has indexes for various subsectors, such as banks, computers, and biotechnology. But an "average" investor is primarily interested in the results of the Nasdaq Composite.

A key difference between the Nasdaq Composite Index and the Dow Jones Averages is that, in the Nasdaq, the relative importance of the stock prices is determined by the value of the shares outstanding. This means that the price of each share is multiplied by the number of shares outstanding to get what is called the total market capitalization of the stock. This means that stocks with higher prices and/or a higher number of shares outstanding carry the most weight in the Nasdaq Index. Because there are so many small stocks in the Nasdaq, the top 100 stocks carry most of the weight, and this is why there is a separate index for the Nasdaq 100.

Since the Nasdaq Composite Index includes all of the stocks presently traded in the Nasdaq market, there are thousands of stocks involved, rather than the 30 of the Dow Jones Average. For example, at the end of 1996, there were 6,384 issues in the Nasdaq Composite. At the time this was the highest number of issues in any index.

The Nasdaq Composite Index, as noted in the text of this book, soared from an initial value of 100 in 1971 to a value of 5,000 in the spring of 2000. This was an increase of over 50 times, but of course after the Nasdaq crash produced over a 60 percent decline in the Index, it stood just below 2,000 for much of the year 2001. The fact that the Nasdaq still has increased by a factor of 20 since its inception, despite its crash, indicates why investors are still interested in the Nasdaq Index. Essentially one can say that the Dow Jones Index reflects the performance of the "old economy" ("bricks-and-mortar" companies) while the Nasdaq reflects the performance of the "new economy," i.e., high technology and internet stocks ("dot.coms"). This may or may not be true, but the real question an investor should ask of an index is whether the stocks it represents are reasonably priced. That, of course, depends on the criteria used to define "reasonable," because the answer to the question lies in the future as the index rises and falls.

Standard & Poor's 500 Index

Standard and Poor's is a financial services company that is essentially in competition with Dow Jones and other such financial service companies. They came up with the Standard & Poor's 500 Index (S&P 500) to compete with the Dow Jones average and to facilitate the selling of their financial services. Standard and Poor's computes several indexes beyond their 500 stock composite. These include the 400 MidCap and the 500 SmallCap, as well as even smaller subsets of the S&P 500, such as the S&P Utilities Index and the S&P Industrials Index. Standard & Poor's even has an additional index called the S&P 100, which was specifically created for the trading of options.

The S&P 500 Composite includes 400 industrial, 40 utility, 20 transportation, and 40 financial stocks. A key difference between the S&P 500 Index and the Dow Jones Averages is that, in the S&P 500, as in the Nasdaq and most other indexes, the relative importance of the stock prices is determined by the value of the shares outstanding. This means that higher-priced stocks and/or stocks with many shares outstanding carry the most weight in the Index. In the case of the S&P 500, such stocks tend to be those of the biggest and most popular companies, and, since the 30 Dow Jones Industrials also are selected from the biggest and most popular companies, it is not so surprising that the Dow Jones and the S&P 500 correlate so well. Anyone who is familiar with statistics will realize that 30 of the biggest and most popular stocks are really a very good sample of the stock market. When you compare the 30 from the Dow Jones Averages with the S&P 500 combined index (which in turn is driven by relatively few of the biggest stocks in the index), you should find very good correlation. As noted above, you do.

The S&P 500 price index was first published on a daily basis in 1957, although some of its other indexes were published before that. Using the ability of computers, it has been extended back to 1928 so that one can get values for the S&P 500 since that date. Because of its broad scope, and the fact that it is weighted by market capitalization, the S&P 500 has become the favored market measure of portfolio managers and scholars from the ivory towers of academia. This is no small thing for the portfolio managers, because their annual bonuses are based on their ability to "beat" the return on the S&P 500. Also, many so-called index funds, which copy the composition of the S&P 500, advertise that their returns are the same of those achieved on the S&P 500. Their advertising falls short in terms of attracting investors if the S&P 500 does not have a very good return. The managers of the S&P 500 constantly replace the stocks that make up the index as the fortunes of the 500 stocks in the index rise and fall. Some brokers even try to guess what stocks may be brought into, and/or thrown out from, the index on the basis that being included will cause the stock price to go up, while being excluded will cause the stock price to decline.

As noted, there are also indexes for the various subsections of the S&P 500 (the 400 industrials, 40 utilities, 20 transportation, and 40 financials). The values for these indexes can be found in various newspapers. However, beyond the S&P 500 Composite Index, probably the next most popular portion of the S&P family of indexes is the S&P MidCap Index. MidCap means stocks that are in the middle bracket of total market capitalization, i.e. a market capitalization of about $1 billion (small capitalization stocks are those well below $1 billion, and large capitalization stocks are those well above $10 billion). The MidCap Index is popular because it indicates the market direction of the middle capitalization stocks, which are popular with investors who want rapid growth but who also want reasonably large companies for stability. The stocks in the S&P 400 MidCap Index are usually larger and more stable than most of the stocks in the Nasdaq Composite.

The Russell 2000 Index

This Index is named after the Frank Russell Company, which is a well known consulting firm in Tacoma, WA that specializes in pension issues. They have developed a number of indexes to use in the performance measurement of money managers who run pension funds. As part of this process, the Russell 2000 Index was developed to compare so-called MidCap companies (those with market capitalization near $1 billion, as noted above when we discussed the S&P 400 MidCap Index).

The Russell 2000 Index represents the smallest two-thirds of the 3,000 largest U.S. companies based on total market capitalization. By definition, two-thirds of 3,000 is 2,000, and thus it is easy to see how the Index got its name. The composition of the Index needs to be revised relatively often, as some companies grow rapidly and some companies stumble. This means that previously smaller companies are constantly migrating upwards to the top one-third, while unsuccessful companies previously in the top one-third are constantly drifting down into the lower two-thirds, just like an unending amount of debris constantly drifts down in the oceans of the world to settle on the bottom. In the same way, the amount of market capitalization that defines "MidCap" generally increases because the number of shares outstanding constantly increases, even through prices can wander up and down.

The first four indexes listed above are by far the most popular indexes used by investors and analysts alike. If you are listening to the network news on either the radio, television, or even internet, they generally have time for only a quick input on how the market did today, and they will give you the values for the Dow Jones Industrials Index and the Nasdaq Composite Index. If you are listening to a local station, they will add the S&P 500 and the Russell 2000 to give you what they feel is a complete picture. They will also occasionally give you the most popular indexes in Tokyo and London, and we will cover those below.

The Wilshire 5000 Index

This index was created in 1974, and it is based on market capitalization, like all of the indexes we have discussed above, with the exception of the Dow Jones Averages. The Wilshire 5000 Index, at the time it was created, claimed to be the broadest stock market index because it included all U.S. based companies with readily available price data. It includes all actively traded stocks on the NYSE, the Nasdaq, and all other stock exchanges. As note above, the Nasdaq Composite Index claimed to have over 6,000 issues in its Index, but over 1,000 of these issues were either foreign, securities, warrants, and other such items (warrants are essentially an option to buy certain stocks). So the Wilshire 5000 may not necessarily be the biggest index at any given time, but it is certainly close to the top, and its criteria of limiting itself to "actively" traded stocks may permit it to maintain its claim.

At any rate, the Wilshire 5000 is certainly close to being the index with the broadest measure of the stock market, and Index funds such as the Vanguard Total Stock Market Index Fund, a well-known mutual fund, tries to replicate all of the stocks in the Wilshire 5000. Unless you have some reason to know what the total market is doing, the Wilshire 5000 would not be of much use for your personal investments, even if it is of use to certain mutual funds.

The NYSE Composite Index

As noted in the text of the Chronology, the NYSE Composite Index was created in 1965. Its creation was supposedly the result of an effort to placate President Johnson, who had been told "no" when he asked the Dow Jones company to revise the Dow Jones Average to, in his words, better reflect the state of the economy. This meant that he thought the Dow Jones Average was making the economy look worse than it was, and he simply wanted to change it so he could take credit for improving the economy. President Johnson was not used to being told "no," and the NYSE decided they had an opportunity to gain some brownie points with the President.

Whether the story is true or not (it certainly has some credibility, knowing the personality of President Johnson), the creation of the NYSE Composite at the time, it was claimed, was the broadest market measure available. The Index is composed of all of the stocks listed on the NYSE. Since the NYSE was by far the biggest stock market in the world at the time, its claim certainly had validity. In the mid 1990s, the number of common stocks listed on the NYSE was more than 2,700, which is more than it had in 1965, but fewer than the indexes represented by both the Nasdaq Composite and the Wilshire 5000.

Like the S&P 500, the NYSE Composite Index has a number of subgroups. These include, not surprisingly, the NYSE Industrials, the NYSE Utilities, and the NYSE Transportation Indexes. The similarity to the Dow Jones family of indexes is quite deliberate. The NYSE also adds an additional subgroup called the NYSE Finance Index. None of these indexes are very popular for use in investing and analyzing, but with the great proliferation of option writers, the NYSE group of indexes gives them some additional vehicles on which to write options. That makes the NYSE indexes an additional source of revenue for option writers.

Incidentally, although the NYSE indexes were not originally developed for the purpose of writing options, this has become a standard practice in today's new marketplace. For example, the American Stock Exchange (AMEX), which used to be a poor second to the NYSE in the stock exchanges in the United States, and which had its own index as far back as 1966, decided to focus on option writing around 1980 because it was obvious it would never compete with the NYSE as a stock exchange. The AMEX was subsequently acquired by the Nasdaq in 1998, and it now is almost entirely an options exchange. Before it was acquired, the AMEX developed about 15 indexes, some of which are very obscure, simply for the purpose of having options written on them. The AMEX has changed greatly since its days as The Curb Exchange in the early 1900s.

The Value Line Composite Average

This index has the advantage of age in the sense that it first appeared in 1963. It also was derived differently than all other averages, using a method known as the geometric relative price changes of the component stocks. It is not necessary to expand on the manner in which it is calculated, except to say it was never an average, and was always a specialized index. In my view, it also has the disadvantage of being associated with the Value Line Company, whose purpose for creating the index was to generate sales for the company's mutual funds.

At its beginning, the Value Line consisted of about 1,400 stocks, and thus was considered as a broad based average. More recently, it contained 1,700 different issues, most of which were listed on the NYSE, but which were secondary stocks rather than the most popular stocks. Because of its heavy inclusion of secondary stocks, the Value Line was cynically considered by stock market analysts as a good measure of what the "typical" investor might be buying. When these analysts said "typical" investor, they meant "less sophisticated" investors, who were usually associated with buying stocks when they had reached market tops, and selling when stocks had reached the bottom.

At any rate, the new indexes like the Russell 2000 and the Nasdaq 100 and the Nasdaq Composite have greatly reduced the value of the Value Line index. Of historical interest is the fact that the Value Line Average was the basis for the first stock index futures contract in 1982, on the Kansas City Board of Trade. The Value Line index is really listed here for completeness. It really is an index of the past, not the present.

London FT-SE 100

This index contains the stocks of Britain's 100 largest companies as ranked by market capitalization, like nearly all of the indexes listed here. It is by far the most widely quoted index for those who track the London stock exchange. Because of its title, it is usually announced on news programs as the "Footsie" 100, and it is one of the international index quotes you will hear on news shows who believe their coverage of the markets is a little above other news shows.

Tokyo Nikkei 225

This index tracks the 225 major issues on the Tokyo stock exchange. It has often been called the "Dow Jones of Japan." Dow Jones actually has a number of international indexes of its own, which have no relation to the Nikkei 225. But the Nikkei 225 might wish it did as well as the Dow Jones has done in the United States.

As we have mentioned in the Introduction, and in this Appendix, the Japanese stock market is the most outstanding (or infamous) example of how stock markets can go bust for a very long time. During the decade of the 1980s, when the economy of Japan was admired in almost every way by Western countries, the Nikkei 225 rose from 12,000 at the beginning of the decade to almost 40,000 in 1989. Many observers claimed that this was a gigantic bubble, supported by the isolationist actions of the Japanese government. At the same time the Nikkei 225 was climbing by a factor of four, real estate values in Tokyo were climbing even faster. These inflated real estate values had a lot to do with the apparent success of the Japanese economy in the 1980s.

At any rate, when the bubble burst in 1989, the Nikkei average started a long descent down from 40,000. It fell below 20,000 in early 1992, and then fell below 15,000 in June 1995. Not satisfied with ruining the retirement hopes of those who retired in 1989, the Nikkei has continued to slide slowly downward, and in the summer of 2001, it was dipping below 12,000. The last time it was so low was more than 17 years ago.

So once again, we can reiterate that stock markets can go down and stay down for a long time. Every time you hear it only happened in the past, like "way back in 1929" (it took the market 25 years to regain the level it reached just before the crash of 1929), you should consider the present state of the Japanese stock market, which may take more that 25 years to recover its past peaks. At any rate, however long it takes, many of the Japanese people who were counting on their stock market to fund their retirement will no longer be with us when their stock market comes back.

7. AXIOMS

There is almost literally no end to the number of axioms about the stock market. The more persons you talk to, the more axioms you can add to your list. As I stated in the Introduction, advice about how to invest is generally avoided in this book. But now that we have seen how the same old errors arise again and again in producing the three spectacular crashes in the last 75 years (1929, 1987, and 2001), I feel that selecting some axioms that have stood the test of time and that could produce a mindset that would protect against the recurrent errors would be a useful addition to this part of the book. I have also tried to indicate the origin of two of the axioms, but I must point out that just as Yogi Berra is endlessly credited with axioms about baseball, the original J.P. Morgan has a similar role in axioms about the stock market. So be it. He deserves more recognition as a truly original thinker about the market.

A bull can make money in Wall Street, and a bear can make money in Wall Street, but a pig never will— This axiom comes in several versions, but the thought is the same, and it is one of the most important thoughts. Careful study and investing can make money for you whether you act as a bull or a bear. But once you get greedy and act as a pig, who always simply wants more, you are on the way out. What this book teaches about greed makes this perhaps the most important axiom.

Never fall in love with a stock— You will hear the same advice about buying a house or a car. Once you are determined to have a specific stock (or house or car), your ability to make a serious judgment about the price you want to pay is gone. This is true for long-term investing as well. No matter how long you have held it, the time will come when another stock is a better investment for your circumstances than the one you hold. Be objective.

A margin call is the most sincere tip you will ever get from your broker—If you deal on margin and your broker makes a margin call, he is telling you without any euphemisms that the time has come to sell. A corollary to this axiom is to *never answer a margin call*, i.e., don't send in any more money to maintain your margin. Let your broker sell the stock and just forget it. The biggest losers in a downturn are people who have lost far more than they ever planned to risk because they bought on margin and kept trying to maintain it. When the margin call comes from your broker, both he and the market are trying very sincerely to tell you something. It's time to go.

Cut your losses and let your profits run—I hesitate to include this one even though it is absolutely true. The problem is that it is a little like the advice to buy low and sell high. If you have the discipline to follow this axiom, you will ideally never suffer any big losses, and most of your stocks always will be above water. Essentially what you are doing with this axiom is letting the market tell you which stocks are good investments at this particular time. The best research you can do (or buy) is not nearly as good as good as what the market will provide. You may sell a good stock too soon, but you can always buy it back later if it still appears to be a good buy in the future. A corollary axiom is *don't fight the market*. When it tells you to sell, sell. The market always gives you objective advice.

The public is always wrong—This may seem a bit cynical, but we have shown clearly in this book that the last stage of every big crash came when the "public" came rushing into a bubble trying to get some easy money. Also, in the past, odd-lot sales (which were then the main vehicle the public used to come into the market) supposedly peaked at market highs and fell at market lows. The key point is that when everyone starts talking about their success in the market and is anxious to give you a hot tip, it's time to get out. Even Charles Dow, the developer of the Dow-Jones average, said at the end of the 1890s that the entry into the market of the general public, as opposed to market professionals, was a bad thing because the public was looking for easy money rather than long time investments.

The market will fluctuate—This is one of the Axioms credited to the original J. P. Morgan. Once in the middle of a developing panic, he was besieged by reporters nearly all of whom were asking the same question, "Mr. Morgan, what will the market do?" His simple answer was, "Gentlemen, it will fluctuate." He was, as he usually was, absolutely correct.

Sell down to the sleeping point—This is another axiom often credited to Morgan, although it has also been credited to others. It is one of my favorites because it embodies what I think is a key point in what should be your overall approach to the stock market. The story is that a friend of Morgan told him in a private conversation that he needed some advice. He told Morgan that he was constantly worried about his stocks and the stock market, and now he was so consumed with worry, he couldn't sleep at night. When he asked plaintively, "What should I do?," Morgan replied simply, "I suggest you sell down to the sleeping point."

As I noted in the introduction, and in some of the prior items here, when you invest in such things as zero-coupon bonds, you have no interest in what the market is doing day-to-day. Your sleep is never interrupted by the machinations of the marketplace.

SELECTED BIBLIOGRAPHY

Alsop, Ronald J., Editor. *The Wall Street Journal Almanac, 1998*. New York: Ballantine Books, 1997.

_____. *The Wall Street Journal Almanac, 1999*. New York: Ballantine Books, 1998.

Brooks, John. *Once in Golconda*. New York: Allworth Press, 1969.

Buck, James E., ed. *The New York Stock Exchange, The First 200 Years*. Essex, Connecticut: Greenwich Publishing Group, Inc., 1992.

Editors of The Wall Street Journal. *Who's and What's What on Wall Street*. New York: Ballantine Books, 1998.

Farrell, Maurice L., Editor. *The Dow Jones Averages 1885–1970*. New York: Dow Jones & Company, Inc., 1972.

Geisst, Charles, R. *Wall Street, A History*. New York: Oxford University Press, 1997.

_____. *100 Years of Wall Street*. New York: McGraw Hill, 2000.

Glassman, James K. and Kevin A. Hassett. *Dow 36,000*. New York: Times Business/Random House, 1999.

Mayer, Martin. *Markets: Who Plays, Who Risks, Who Gains, Who Loses*. New York: W.W. Norton & Company, 1988.

McGeveran, William A. Jr., Editorial Director. *The World Almanac, 2001*. Mahaw, New Jersey: World Almanac Books, 2001.

Parrillo, Douglas, F., Editor. *The Nasdaq Handbook*. Chicago: Probus Publishing Company, 1987.

Pierce, Phyllis, Editor. *The Dow Jones Averages 1885–1995*. New York: Dow Jones & Company, Inc., 1996.

Teweles, Richard J. and Edward S. Bradley. *The Stock Market, 7th Edition*. New York: John Wiley & Sons, Inc., 1998.

Wendt, Lloyd. *The Wall Street Journal*. Chicago: Rand McNally & Company, 1982.

INDEX